Calling After Water

CALLING AFTER WATER

Dispatches from a Fishing Life

DAVE KARCZYNSKI

FOREWORD BY TOM BIE

Essex, Connecticut

An imprint of The Globe Pequot Publishing Group, Inc.
64 South Main Street
Essex, CT 06426
www.globepequot.com

Distributed by NATIONAL BOOK NETWORK

British Library Cataloguing in Publication Information available

Library of Congress Cataloging-in-Publication Data

Names: Karczynski, Dave, 1980- author.
Title: Calling after water : dispatches from a fishing life / by Dave
    Karczynski ; foreword by Tom Bie.
Description: Essex, Connecticut : Lyons Press, [2024]
Identifiers: LCCN 2024023036 (print) | LCCN 2024023037 (ebook) | ISBN
    9781493086467 (cloth) | ISBN 9781493086474 (ebook)
Subjects: LCSH: Fly fishing—Anecdotes. | Trout fishing—Anecdotes. |
    Karczynski, Dave, 1980-
Classification: LCC SH456 .K268 2024 (print) | LCC SH456 (ebook) | DDC
    799.12/4—dc23/eng/20240617
LC record available at https://lccn.loc.gov/2024023036
LC ebook record available at https://lccn.loc.gov/2024023037

For Amber and Summer

Contents

Foreword by Tom Bie xi

Preface xv

CHAPTER 1: Kidney Country 1

CHAPTER 2: North by North 11

CHAPTER 3: Mad Men 25

CHAPTER 4: Cloud, Castle, Creek 35

CHAPTER 5: Why I Do Muskie Camp 49

CHAPTER 6: In Patagonia 53

CHAPTER 7: Anglers on a Train 67

CHAPTER 8: The San River: A Love Story 77

CHAPTER 9: The Middle Fork of Stupid Good 93

CHAPTER 10: Kings of the Road 105

CHAPTER 11: Vision Quest 111

CHAPTER 12: Debonair Dirtbag 119

CHAPTER 13: Life of Chum 133

CHAPTER 14: Into the Mystic 137

CHAPTER 15: Catching on the Kanektok 147

CHAPTER 16: Now I Lay Me 157

CHAPTER 17: Why We Bass 169

CONTENTS

Chapter 18: A Hex upon Me 179

Chapter 19: So Long on Long Island 189

Acknowledgments 207

Take almost any path you please, and ten to one it carries you down in a dale, and leaves you there by a pool in the stream. There is magic in it. Let the most absent-minded of men be plunged in his deepest reveries—stand that man on his legs, set his feet a-going, and he will infallibly lead you to water, if water there be in all that region. Should you ever be athirst in the great American desert, try this experiment, if your caravan happen to be supplied with a metaphysical professor. Yes, as every one knows, meditation and water are wedded for ever.

—HERMAN MELVILLE, *MOBY DICK*

Foreword

Dave Karczynski is a troll. Not in the internet scrum-scrolling way, but as someone who lives under (south of) Michigan's Mackinac Bridge, which connects the state's Upper and Lower Peninsulas. I know this because, after publishing one of Dave's earlier essays—a 2013 story about fishing along Michigan's M-72 highway—one of his many fans emailed me to point out that I had incorrectly identified what is and is not Michigan's U.P. The offended reader shared that he was a native "Yooper" (those living north of the Mackinac Bridge) and he seemed mildly disappointed that Karczynski was not a fellow member of the Yooper class. I diagnose this as a clear indication of early onset fanboy: readers wanting to claim Karczynski as one of their own. Do not be surprised when Dave's laptops are someday displayed atop bare tables in countless Midwest museums à la Hemingway's writing desks stretching from Sun Valley to Walloon Lake to Havana.

Karczynski's readers have good reason for reverence. Especially the anglers. His writing mimics the splendid variety of a smallmouth eat, at times coming straight at you—fast, bold, efficient—getting right to the point with the fewest words possible. Other times, his sentences are like a slow follow on an early spring day, when the anticipatory buildup is as rewarding as the conclusion itself. He describes everything—flowers, bushes, grasses, rocks, mammals, and of course fish. On pike: "It is the perfect weapon, bow and arrow in a single package."

Troll or not, culturally, Karczynski is a true northerner: part char, part *Esox*; good with a canoe, axe, or filet knife; knows how to build a campfire or start an old Evinrude; is a competent gear-chucker if need be; most comfortable chasing northerns, brookies, muskie, walleye, and smallmouth; knows the value of following a two-track; eats cheese curds; owns plenty of flannel. The kind of guy that, if he operated a backhoe for a living, you'd see drinking a beer, shirtless, at a Packers game in November. As a fly-fishing writer, he wears earmuffs, three sweaters, and a puffy, but you get the point. He understands that angling etiquette changes when chasing difficult boreal fish. On muskie: "If you get lucky once, you revel, and if you get lucky twice, you row."

It's a rare talent to make a unique experience feel relatable to a reader. But it's harder still to describe the commonplace in an unconventional way. Karczynski excels at both. I once wrote an intro for my magazine about the struggles of stringing a rod properly while trout are actively feeding all around you. Dave describes a similar scene in which he suspects that smallies may be tempted into a surface eat: "The only presentation outfit I had, a 6-weight with floating line, was still in its tube. But it was time. My hands were not my own as I started fitting the ferrules together. They weren't shaking, exactly, but they were also not firmly under my control. I have always called this phenomenon 'hatch hands,' and they only happen when there is a deep certainty that fishing joy is imminent."

The most quoted rule in writing comes from E. B. White's *Elements of Style*: "A sentence should contain no unnecessary words." Despite my years of carpet-bombing freelancers with White's sage advice, Karczynski reminds us that even this most sacred decree can be broken by those with the skills to do so. The serviceable author omitting needless words writes: "I had plenty of fly-tying material." Karczynski writes: "I was exceedingly wealthy in fly-tying materials, with a particularly robust portfolio of elk and moose assets, in addition to my ample rooster holdings." This clever, longer description wasn't "necessary" just as it wasn't necessary for *Shawshank Redemption* to include Andy Dufresne's long crawl through the shit-pipe. But it made for a far better movie.

One of Karczynski's special talents is highlighted when he fishes abroad. He is uniquely gifted at acknowledging the joy and wonder of travel while simultaneously expressing his longing for the comfortable familiarity of his home water. He has roamed extensively—Poland, Chile, Alaska, Labrador—yet he knows how to articulate the tradeoff: "No matter how good the day at one of these far-flung destinations had been, when I went to bed each night I was haunted by what I was missing back home in Michigan: giant, demon-eyed trout with spots as big as your fist; moonlit mudflats that went from calm to bubbling in the blink of an eye; the baritone *thunk* of a big trout rising in the dark, so resonant you could feel it in your chest, like a grouse's wingbeat."

Humor can be hard to pull off in writing, especially if you aren't funny. And super-especially if you aren't funny and believe that you are funny. Karczynski uses just the right amount of humor, often at his own expense, using humility and self-deprecation. He doesn't overdo it, doesn't force it, and he finds opportunities to lighten the mood when you least expect it. Like during real trouble, when he'd badly injured his foot on a remote canoe trip, forcing his brother to shuttle the entire load solo to the next camp: "I felt deep guilt and wished I'd written out some sort of angler's will, a document to make clear that, if a bear or cougar dispatched me before I reached the lake, my brother was entitled to a full day of relaxed fishing before feeling any obligation to pack out my remains."

Karczynski has a habit of turning nouns like *bugs* and *fish* into verbs. ("I haven't hexed in five years." "Why we bass.") This speaks to how deeply rooted fishing has become in his life, and your own love of fishing—fly fishing especially—is likely why you are holding this book in the first place. I also love fly fishing, but the real beauty of *Calling After Water* comes down to exceptional storytelling.

This is the result not just of good writing, but of ruthless, relentless rewriting—reviewing and revising each sentence until it has a rhythm and flow that can't even be adequately described. Dave just knows it when he sees it. He doesn't just fix "bad" sentences, he takes already great sentences and intuitively knows they can be better. And he makes them better. Enjoy this book and enjoy your fishing.

—Tom Bie

Preface

I have always written and I have always fished, though not in the forms I have come to practice both arts. For the first half of my life, when I fished it was with conventional tackle. When I wrote, it was fiction. The two practices never met; through none of the thousands of pages I wrote swam one single fish.

Then one year in my mid-20s I won a large cash prize to finish a half-done novel. Some of the money I used to buy waders and a fly rod. Wouldn't it be fun and relaxing to tinker with a new form of fishing while I wrapped up the novel? That was my innocent thinking at the time.

Little did I know this decision would start a conflict of epic proportions.

"I can't stop fishing long enough to make any progress on the book," I told a fellow writer during one of our regular gripe-fests at the pub. "Actually, I might be going backwards. Whenever I sit down to a blank page, all I see are trout."

"Why not write about fishing?" she said.

I sat back, stunned. I made her repeat the question three times. It was a bizarre idea to me at the time—to find one's material not in some dusty corner of the mind but sitting there at your feet—or, in my case, flowing around my knees. To write not about some invented land full of made-up people but about something that had actually happened to you. To write, further, about an activity that you loved.

I tried it—and the words flowed like a river after a winter thaw. They bubbled up from bottomless secret springs. Writing about fish and fishing became the easiest, most effortless, most joyful writing that I had ever done. I gave up fiction entirely, and am happy to report that I haven't suffered true writer's block since 2008 (though just as with fishing, there are slow days).

The nineteen essays in this collection take place over roughly fifteen years. In the first, I am a new trout angler in my mid-20s. In the last, I am all of 40 years old and standing—a little tardily, my mother would say—on the threshold of fatherhood. In between are adventures I never thought I'd have, and fish I never dreamed of catching. And though the essays are situated more or less in chronological order, they are not narratively connected. Take, therefore, any approach you please. Read them upstream or down. Step methodically through the run, or cast only at good rises.

I hope that you will like these essays. Assembling them has been a deeply rewarding experience, a chance to relive some of my favorite moments from both my travels and opposite-of-travels. But the thing that strikes me most looking back on these fifteen years—fifteen years during which I fished with my hair on fire—is not the amount of fishing I did, but all the millions of moments I never wrote about. There are only a few hundred words devoted to the muskellunge, a species that has taken years off the life of my rotator cuff. And there is scarce more space devoted to the smallmouth bass, whose company I have enjoyed above that of all other fish. I suppose what I mean to say is that these essays, like any fishing narratives, represent but a small part of a larger whole, a single flake of snow on the tip of the iceberg, or the handful of sputtering mayfly duns among the thousands of nymphs down below. Maybe I'll one day manage to write it all down, encapsulate the entire iceberg, wing every bug. Maybe, but probably not. There's just too much fishing to do.

CHAPTER 1

Kidney Country

I WAS YOUNG. I WAS FREE. AND I WAS SCREWED.

Below me, in the gin-gimlet pool, the trout rose again. He was eighteen inches if he was eight, and in a tight spot. A snarl of branches formed the canopy above him, a limestone cliff pressed in tight just across. I stood chin-high in prairie grass, parting milkweed for a better view. The hatch was plain: Mayflies, frail as vapor, wafted up and off the film. Not plain was how to execute a backcast or rollcast—any cast, really. No, without a well-trained hummingbird to personally deliver my fly, there was no way I was reaching water, let alone a feeding lane.

But I didn't cease or desist. Instead I rubbed my temples, studied my fly box, sipped some bourbon, and said a prayer, pausing from time to time to watch my fish tipple his lunch. I had no clue what to do with him.

What I did have was time. A lot of time. Fresh out of an MFA program in fiction writing, during which time I had published a single one-page story in an obscure literary journal, I was spending the summer holed up in my parents' Wisconsin cottage, waiting, I told everyone, for my "next move." What it was I couldn't say, but with faith in my fiction-writer powers of observation, I knew I would recognize it when the time came. It would descend triumphantly from the sky, ablaze in glorious raiments. Until it did I would live, unablaze and without raiments, in a small cottage in cow country where there were canned beans in the cupboards and landlords who would not evict me. Here I would write and do what I had been wanting to do for years—learn to fly-fish.

The house was located in the heart of the Sand Counties, a region made famous by the writer and conservationist Aldo Leopold and infamous by the trout that lived there. They were products of their environment, and that environment ranged from difficult to impossible from an angler's point of view. With its slow water clear as paint thinner; its bright, sandy bottoms; its narrow, alder-choked banks, it was largely regarded as pass-over country—better to swerve southwest to the Driftless or power through to the freestoners up North. It was not the place for a clueless beginner with an eBay rod and YouTube skills. But that's exactly who I was. With a good pulse of wind to straighten my leader, I could bomb out a cast to maybe twenty-five feet. Decent dead drifts were accidents of wind and current, enacted through no fault of my own. I didn't yet know what a mend was but nonetheless performed them—in jerky spasms as I flicked ticks off my arm. But here, before the largest trout I had ever seen, I had a chance at redemption. Taking this fish would recast the past month in a happy, glowing, fishful light. I could call myself a trout angler and mean what I said.

The time for the cast had come. I managed the first miracle—that of getting my fly into motion without hanging up in front of me—then the second—of finding some open prairie for my backcast. The line fired forward. The Adams dutifully followed. It lashed the branch and stuck fast.

Down below, the trout rose again, oblivious and joyful.

"Dammit!" I yelled. The tree belched my fly on the second hard rip, along with an upchuck of leaves. I cussed and grumbled my way back to the car. For someone with endless free time and minimal obligations, I was a troubled, troubled man.

~•~

I stashed my fly rod for a few days in order to solve the issue theoretically, concluding that my lack of success could not be a skill problem—I had watched too much YouTube for that. It had to be the rod. I couldn't say whether it was too long or too short, too heavy or too light, but it was clearly insufficient. The problem was that I had no money for a new rod. No actual money, anyways. What I did have was a credit card I had never used, its virgin-white activation sticker still intact.

This, however, was not an emergency.

Two Hamms later, I finished the thought: Or was it?

Via a river of faulty logic and the kind semantic violence I had perfected in graduate school, I eventually arrived at the position that this was, in fact, an emergency—and the card lost its innocence. Driving to the nearest fly shop, I decided that since I didn't have any job prospects, I would limit myself to what I could pay back on an autumn's worth of casual plasma donation, say, $150.

The shop was a little over an hour away, deep in Green Bay Packer country. Holding court that day was a pensive older fellow named Jim who I would later learn was the founder of a furled leader company, an early proponent of Tenkara, and a brook trout aficionado, though at that time I did not know what a furled leader was, would have ordered a Tenkara with my sushi, and had the internet to thank for knowing what a brook trout looked like. It being a quiet day in the shop, I spoke in detailed, pidgin fly-speak of my spring creek quandaries, of the rising fish I could not seem to catch, of my growing infatuation with diminutive water.

Jim nodded. "You need something made of magic," he said. "Come with me."

Now it's true that I was not wise in the ways of the fly-fishing world, but I did have enough sense to know that items made of magic tend to cost a pretty penny. When I opened my mouth to explain my financial straits, however, nothing came out. Jim carried about him a hallowed, priestly air, and I felt the invocation of something as crude as money would have been met with instant excommunication from a circle I desperately sought to enter.

"A rod," he gestured calmly, "is your sole ambassador to the watery realm. It must be fluent in a multitude of languages, and know equally the merits of finesse and force." He lifted a glossy, slim rod delicately from the rack and held it forth at eye level, like a sommelier showboating a pedigreed Bordeaux. I squinted at the butt section—not much thicker than a pencil—and read the letters flourished across the blank: 8 foot. 3 weight. I sniffed the cork.

"Let's take it out back," Jim said.

From the moment I took it into my hands I knew that I was dealing with something amazing, something exceptional, something no legal schedule of plasma donation was going to cover. My eBay rod, it became suddenly clear, had been a corpse, a piece of zombie graphite, empty and infected and dead. In contrast this thing I held in my hands, this lithe, lissome entity that Jim called a rod but I recognized as a truer and purer extension of my arm, was alive, tremulous, immortal. Through its guides the line fed like so much spun butter, and when I flung it forth it had a discernible loop—as prophesied by my YouTube mentors. The cast was also endless, relatively speaking—the tuft of pink yarn fell just short of an old lawnmower I was aiming for, a full forty feet away.

"It's nice," I whisper-quavered. "How much would it set me back?"

Jim let fly a number I would have likelier associated with a Boeing passenger jet than a fly rod, so bulky I was surprised it had fit in his mouth. This was no plasma deal. We were in kidney country now.

"Thanks for letting me try it," I said, handing the rod back. It was not the stick for me. I knew the lifestyle I'd led in grad school. I'd be needing doubles of all internal organs down the road.

"It's a beautiful day," he said, pushing the rod back. "At least enjoy some casting. I'll be back inside when you're done."

I shrugged. Jim was right: It *was* a nice day. And there didn't appear to be any danger of breaking the rod, so why not? Swishing about in the sunlight, I forgot about my tenuous future, my many incomplete projects, my artistic penury. Instead I laid out line beneath imaginary bridges, delivered caddis between the branches of make-believe sweepers, made casts through impossibly narrow chutes in sky-high prairie grass. I focused so intently I saw riseforms dilating in the shade of the hedges. Mayflies were coming off, and I landed three nice browns in succession. They were beautiful fish, ablaze in crimson-speckled raiments.

I froze.

Ablaze . . . in . . . raiments.

I remember only scraps of what happened next. There was the unsticking of my credit card from the tightest recess of wallet. There were handshakes, slaps on the back. A complimentary spool of fly line. May air on my face. The blurred white lines of the highway.

I came to about halfway home, chest tight, mouth dry. Glancing at my reflection in the rearview, I met the gaze of a young man with a suddenly much more tentative grip on his organs. Behind him, sitting upright in the back seat, was a deep-green cylinder wearing a glittering gold cap.

My next move was even wearing his seat belt.

⚊•⚊

I remember the next few days as quiet, somber. Back at my parents' cottage, I fulfilled all my squatter's duties with a grave penitence, meticulously weeding the garden, mowing each inch of lawn, picking every errant pebble off the cobbled pathway. My utterly foolish, absolutely unaccountable purchase never left its protective case. It was not too late to return it. These things had to happen all the time.

But I didn't return it. Nor did I uncap it. It just lay leaning in a corner next to the door. A fixture. A warning. A temptation.

One day, following a particularly lonely, particularly unproductive bout of writing, I decided to give the rod another look. Carefully, tenderly, I extracted each segment from its cloth slip and laid them out on the kitchen table. Soft afternoon light was falling, and the stick glowed like a sin ripe for the making. What was it Jim had said as he handed it over to me? That I'd give this rod to my grandchildren one day? I'd need a girlfriend first, and probably a job at some point—neither portended by the rural Wisconsin stars. Then I had a thought of an entirely different order. Was it possible that in buying this astronomically expensive rod I had actually done a smart thing? That the debt incurred might act as a kind of incentive to kick my life into gear? I quorumed a trio of Hamms, who made it clear to me that in fact I couldn't afford *not* to keep this rod, representing as it did an era—no, a lifetime—of productivity.

So that's the way it went down, with me filling out the warranty card before falling asleep among my empty aluminum advisors, with me driving out to the post office as soon as it opened the next morning, with me stopping at the local diner on the way home to revise my game plan for the rest of the summer. The most important change: Fishing would be rebranded from a *distraction from hard writing* to a *reward for hard writing*. And just to make things totally unambiguous I itemized twelve distinct writing benchmarks worthy of a fishing reward, drawing little empty boxes next to each item on the list. When one got Xed, I could go fishing. And if you had come up to me right there and told me that I would be on the water that very evening battling my first twenty brook trout through a Brown Drake spinner fall, that my "game plan" would be the last writing I would do for months, that the garden would go wild, my novel defunct, my voice-mail unchecked; if you were to tell me at that moment that I would spend most of the rest of my summer days not in my parents' cottage but in my orange tent beside any number of rivers, enjoying hot beans for dinner, cold beans for breakfast, and heartburn for lunch; if you had told me any of these things I would have smugly shaken my head and said: "Shows how well you know me."

＊＊＊

One morning in mid-August I was fishing what had come to be my favorite river, a lazy spring creek very absent of anglers and very full of brook trout, a place I had dubbed "the Brookies Institute." During previous trips I had caught several fish in the twelve-inch range and was confident I'd missed a few larger. In this spot the fish all tended to hole up in a deep pool with a sweeper, so many fish the bare tree looked heavily foliaged. If you were very careful, once you got within range you could catch them one after another, plucking the tree bare.

I ghosted to within view of the pool, looking for my familiar brookies, but instead saw a fish that jellied my knees and churned the beans in my gut: an absolutely massive brown trout.

I had never seen a trout this large with my own eyes, and the site of it amongst the brookies gave it a grotesque appearance with its hooked salmonoid beak, the humped muscles of its shoulders, its spots the size of nickels. The only way to grow this large in a place this small was to eat the neighbors one by one. I estimated it to be somewhere in the vicinity of thirty inches. I looked at the rod in my hand and sighed. There was no way my 3-weight had the power to land this fish.

I stood staring for three of four eternities. Fish shuffled and reshuffled positions at the head of the hole. Several fleets of clouds came and went. At last I hazarded a cast, a sloppy cast that landed much too hard on the water. The brookies burst the branches like a murder of crows, but Leviathan lagged a touch behind, lurching from one end of the pool to the other like an enormous pinball. Because there was nowhere for it to go—the riffles above and below the pool were impassable trickles—it made a ridiculously comical attempt at hiding in some tree branches, an atavistic impulse from the days when it was not the size of an elephant. Then I stepped forward, and it did what I did not think it could do: launch its nightmarish bulk through the inch-deep riffle that formed the downstream boundary of the pool, cleaving more air than water as it disappeared around a downstream bend.

I sat for a long time on the bank. Whatever spell I had been under that summer was broken. I no longer wanted to fish for the little brookies I had caught all season. I wanted to chase large trout. For that, I'd need different gear. And a lot more time. Suddenly I was no longer the emperor of the spring creeks but a guy in his 20s without money or a job, and only a few weeks of trout season left in the calendar.

Back at the cottage that night, I beheld the extent of my dereliction. The garden had gone to seed several times over; zucchini shriveled on the vine; the mailbox barfed envelopes and fliers. I panicked: How much money would I need to get out West? What skills or services could I swap for a floor to sleep on? The answer: none. In any case winter was coming, and these were summer plans. My only choice was to return to the job-application process. As I sifted through the pile of mail, I crafted résumé summaries in my head: "Work-averse guy with useless degree seeks job in bad economy."

Going through the flimsy fliers, something stood out—a thick, stiff letter bearing the logo of the University of Michigan. I remembered that, many weeks ago in a rare moment of maturity, I had filled out an application for an adjunct teaching position. My heart stuttered as I ripped it open. Rejections letters were not this thick.

I was offered a one-semester lectureship teaching freshman composition. Four months of work with benefits. The pay was low by human standards, astronomical by mine. I signed the acceptance letter, then drove it out to the post office.

There was a little more oxygen in the air as I took the long way home down the county roads. I watched the sun dropping behind old wooden barns and thought through my classes, what essays I'd teach, what assignments I'd give. Before heading back to the cottage, I stopped at the Citgo station, the only internet for miles. I sat down with my laptop at an empty table and started to study Michigan's rivers. There was trout water, so much trout water, not right in Ann Arbor, but also not that far away. Within a four-hour drive there lay the Au Sable, the Manistee, the Pere Marquette. Farther north flowed the Jordan, the Boardman, the Black. And there were stretches of water, even entire rivers, where the season never ended. I held that entire blue-veined peninsula of promise in my head as I lay me down to sleep that night. And as my eyes closed and brain slowed, I fished all that sweet unknown water that lay ahead of me. I fished hex and Hendricksons. I landed steelhead and salmon. I threw mice at midnight and twitched grasshoppers at noon. And then I swam off into dreams.

CHAPTER 2

North by North

IF THE WATER WAS COLD, I DIDN'T FEEL IT.

I didn't feel any vertigo, either, even though I'd caught up to the canoe where the lake bottom drops out from 30 to 150 feet deep. At the very least I should have felt relief for having overtaken the vessel in the first place, given we were camped on an island far from shore just after ice-out, in an area so remote we hadn't seen even a float plane for days. But I felt none of these things. Grabbing the gunwale and swimming the canoe back to shore, everything was obliterated by the pain in my foot.

"I just reacted," I told my brother after I slithered up on shore, wincing at the golf-ball swelling on my right foot, like a second, bigger, purpler ankle. The morning had been uncannily calm—water flat as glass, spruces deathly still. Then, out of nowhere, a rogue gust had snatched our canoe from its rock perch, flung it skyward, and kited it out to sea. The rest happened in a blur. One moment I was beside the campfire, the next I was in the water. Somewhere in between, in the rush down the embankment, I must have caught my ankle.

"I can't believe I forgot to tie it down," Jeff said. "I've never forgotten to tie it down."

"I shouldn't have moved so fast," I replied. "I should have chosen my footing better."

I stuck my foot back in the water. The cold bite of the lake helped the pain a little, but it did nothing for the sick feeling in my stomach. I knew what a broken foot would mean out here in the bush: no private paradise of lake trout and walleye and northern pike; no sweet life of shore lunches and campfires; no aching muscles and blistered hands and the blind deep sleep that knitted you back together by sunrise. No, a broken ankle on the route we had chosen—our hardest, deepest trek in the twenty years we'd been doing this—would mean removing the satellite phone from its little Pelican case, opening the Scotch that was supposed to last us all week, sitting at the water's edge and waiting for a rescue plane.

"See if you can put weight on it," Jeff said.

I stood up and slowly started to rock on my foot with gentle pressure. There was a danger, I knew, in misdiagnosis. An angler dealt a broken ankle at the start of a fishing trip could, through sheer willpower, convince themselves that it was just a sprain—to catastrophic effect. Earlier that year I'd read an essay by the British fishing writer Arthur Ransome, who wrote of how his father had suffered a fall at the outset of a trout expedition and decided, since the weather was perfect and the flows just right, to delay treatment. He fished for a week, the ankle got worse, he caught gangrene and died.

I did not want to catch gangrene and die.

At the same time, I didn't want to abandon a trip my brother and I had talked about for four years, almost pulled off twice, and had now just started. A trip for which my brother had told a five-hundred-mile lie to his wife (she thought we were farther south in more familiar country) and for which I'd taken an unpaid leave of absence from work (sometimes the only way to take two weeks off in the middle of the spring semester is to skip the spring semester).

And so after a few more minutes I stood up and grabbed the paddle, stabbed it into rock, and took two foal-like steps forward. The pain was only totally unbearable if I put pressure square on my foot. If I only used the edge, the pain was only somewhat unbearable.

"We have Advil and duct tape?" I asked.

Jeff nodded.

"Then we should probably get breakfast going," I said, limping toward the fire. "And then we should probably fish."

⌒⌒

Ask anyone who's done serious time in canoe country and they'll tell you that some people just don't make it out of the woods with their relationships intact. In the backcountry, every gesture represents who you are as a person, each stroke of the paddle and rod of the portage brings you closer and closer to your core being. By the time you break camp on the final day, you are who you are: greedy or selfless, lazy or dutiful, a valued member of your own small society or an insufferable ass-hat. Forget Myers-Briggs: The only tools you need for self-divination are a paddle, a hatchet, and eighty miles of empty Canadian Shield.

My brother and I had had plenty of time to vet our compatibility. We'd been plying water together since the early 1980s in the south suburbs of Chicago, a largely industrial landscape where fishing was mostly ill-advised and catching anything decent was next to impossible. Yet we persevered, hitting water retention systems, decorative ponds in churchyards, and those artificial lakes with lights and fountains that sit in the middle of apartment complexes. Then our father started taking us North, or what passed for North at the time—deep enough into Wisconsin for taxidermied animals in the grocery store to make perfect sense, but not so deep that we couldn't make it there and back on a three-day weekend.

Then when we were 14 and 15, our high school organized a trip to Minnesota's Boundary Waters Canoe Area, a full week of fishing glory for which nothing in our past could prepare us. Twenty walleye days. Thirty smallmouth in a single morning. Pike that moved so fast to your tube jigs they papercut your eyes. The trip gave my brother and me lifelong scars but the good kind, the opposite of PTSD. Back in Chicago I'd open the juniper jar on the spice rack and huff the scent whenever I needed a break from the gray darkness of a Midwestern winter, whenever I needed to feel the ethereal glow of the rock-rimmed, blue-shimmering North.

We started organizing our own trips and went every year during college and beyond, sometimes with crews as large as eight, but never, for safety reasons, fewer than four. Then five years ago we suspended our trips, way leading on to way. My brother made vice president at a global bank, moved to New York City, got engaged. I took a teaching position that gave me plenty of time to fish, if not much money for anything else.

And now we were back in the North, and for the first time it was just the two of us, here where the roads ended and the caribou began and the only way forward was by paddle or plane. But what, I wondered, did this excursion represent? Was it a capstone trip, the end of an era, a place from which to look back on three decades of fishing and toast to a job well done? Or was it some new beginning, a gateway to even farther-flung destinations: the Hudson Bay tributaries, the Yukon, Nunavut? Would we be content to sit back and admire our accomplishments, or find ourselves admitting there was still work to be done?

— ⌣ —

"This one's a good fish," my brother said, his rod bending in a good arc. "Eight feet down, same as the last one." The lake trout came up, a hungry, lean, early spring fish that we added to two others for a shore lunch. Whatever else lay before us, we had timed the beginning of our trip perfectly. The lake trout were still in their spring patterns—if you could even call it spring. To this land the spring birds hadn't yet returned, and not a single mosquito or blackfly buzzed about. The quiet was compounded by the fact that we were fishing the lee of a large island and there was no wind, no lapping water, no rustling trees. When you stopped paddling and held your breath, your ears felt less empty of sound than full of a thick soundlessness, as if you'd pumped your skull full of caulking foam. Lacking an important sensory dimension, the lake took on a surreal quality, as if it wasn't the world but some panoramic facsimile, a simulation of the universe with a shorted circuit that we paddled into.

We left the quiet of the cove for the main lake, picking up a gentle west wind. Sitting in the back of the canoe, my brother kept us moving smoothly and silently along a variety of barely detectable lake seams—wind-borne microcurrents, subtle algae curtains, drop-offs where the water went from deep to very deep—and I was reminded that in the right hands a canoe is not a vessel to fish from but a tool to fish with. We caught lakers just a few feet below the surface, sometimes in water we had just paddled over. Often we would see them eat. I was fishing a two-streamer rig on a full sinking line, and with each strip of hand or pulse of paddle it looked like two baitfish chasing each other through a blue wilderness of speckled light. You knew you had a fish when one orb of white stopped and the other disappeared.

I was proud of my laker box, which consisted of fly versions of the best lake-trout lures from that first part of my life before I took up the fly rod, a path my brother had had zero interest in following for the very sensible reason that he didn't want to be suddenly very bad at something he was very, very good at—fishing. More of a masochist, and with a good deal more free time, I had pushed through several years of very cumbersome angling and had finally emerged on the other side; with a fly rod I could now hold my own against a very competent gear angler, and sometimes even outfish them. If my brother and I ever started our own fishing business, we'd have all the bases covered. This was an idea I thought about a lot. Even more than a lot. In fact, I secretly harbored a fantasy where, on the last day of this trip, while sipping Scotch around the campfire, Jeff would turn to me and say, "Screw it. This is what we should be doing." He'd leave his job in Manhattan, cash out his retirement, and we'd embark on our true destinies—just like another pair of Chicago fishing brothers, the Lindners.

Whether or not that came to pass, the fishing now was good, even better than good, and we spent two full days chasing aggressive char. Laker afternoons became laker evenings, laker evenings became laker mornings, and all our hot meals became lake-trout feasts. Each fish we caught or ate brought us closer to that fundamental element their flesh expressed and which they had in greater supply than we ever would—freedom. They required no water filters or firewood or hats for the sun. They had no dry bags filled to barfing with extra layers, needed no tents or tarps or rain jackets to avert hypothermia in the cold, wet boreal spring. For a change of residence they simply dipped their noses and made a few sharp tail thrusts, no possibility of spraining a fin. And perhaps most unlike us, they did not have to decide between a life that kept you most free and a life that kept you most fed.

Then one morning when even our sleeping bags smelled like lake trout and it took three slow cups of coffee to surface from our dreams, Jeff asked if I could handle a portage.

"How serious?"

"Somewhat serious."

"What's there?"

"Walleye that haven't been fished to for years."

The next day we were back on the trail, by which I mean that my brother was switchbacking up a jagged hill with the canoe while I limped behind like an elderly wizard, picking my way over rock and using my paddle as a cane. I was grateful that the path to this lake passed through the scorched barrens of a recent fire; even as I fell far behind, I could keep an eye on my brother as he forged ahead, a yellow canoe floating over the burnt hills. When he wordlessly lapped me to grab my gear, I felt deep guilt and wished I'd written out some sort of angler's will, a document to make clear that if a bear or cougar dispatched me before I reached the lake, my brother was entitled to a full day of relaxed fishing before any obligation to pack out my remains.

By the time the old wizard arrived, Jeff had rigged the rods and configured the canoe for fishing. Before setting out we studied a map of the lake, a bizarre watershed shaped like several octopi tied in a knot, all fingers and islands, dead ends and false passages. On top of this baseline treachery, the spines of burn-out jack pine loomed ominously from charred cliffs, and I felt like we were astronauts stranded on some inhospitable planet. In my daydreams of fishing other worlds, the imagery is always idyllic, colorful, and wistful, a cross between a New Zealand fever dream and a Grateful Dead concert, where gold-plated trout swim in green rivers under purple skies. But as we paddled into the walleye sanctuary, it occurred to me that it would probably look more like this: a maze of black water soaking through burnt rock over which you might see a wolf pack—or some extraterrestrial lupine equivalent—loping toward you from a mile away.

We were tired when we started fishing, but that didn't last long. On a backcountry canoe trip there are two ways of warding off the omnipresent fatigue that swarms around you like a cloud of blackflies. One is food followed by sleep followed by food again. The other is great fishing, which we had that day, not necessarily for large fish but for many fish, healthy fish, aggressive fish. It was the kind of day where you start conducting experiments: How big a fly will these walleye take? How fast can you fish one? Can I get one to eat a popper midday? After a few hours of fishing I had my answers—very big, very fast, and almost, almost, almost.

Though we hadn't planned on eating fish that afternoon, we started to get hungry and went ashore to make a primitive lunch. We cut the boughs of some young spruce to serve as a grate and left them to soak in the water as we fileted the fish and made a stove out of rocks. Then we got a good driftwood fire going, and once it burned down to coals, placed the spruce boughs over the rocks and the walleye over the spruce. Watching the sap sizzle and fillets pucker I had the kind of clarity of purpose I've only ever known on a backcountry canoe trip. Here I can see life for what it is. The catching of a fish becomes the eating of a fish. The effort you put into collecting firewood becomes the heat and duration of your fire. The strength of your paddle stroke becomes the length of the glide of your canoe. At home, by contrast, I can sit in front of a keyboard, tap, tap, tap it ten thousand times in my underwear, and via the magic of money this effort may become any number of things: a weeklong cruise, a mountain bike, a slab of sushi-grade tuna. Not in canoe country. Here every relation between action and consequence is direct, no imagination required, no funny business allowed. And while I am sure there are other routes to this sort of clarity and the calm it instills, I personally have not found them outside of the Canadian Shield, or beyond the gunwales of a canoe.

~━━

Our next camp relocation had to wait, since the walleye portage put my ankle out of commission for a few days. But when I was once again capable of hobbling from tree to tree, we struck out on what would be our last major foray, a journey to one of the region's pure pike lakes. It was a perfect way to end the trip. A two-day *Esox* sojourn would ensure our adventure ended on the highest of high notes. It was also a return to the primordial family soup from which my brother and I had slithered, since we come from pike people on both sides. And though our father may have taught us how to fish, it was the pike that taught us cunning.

After five miles of paddling mixed in with a few medium-length portages, we set our final camp on a high bluff overlooking a dark, silty bay. Compared to the earlier lakes, this one was older, shallower, weedier, and in all ways more pikey. After a quick lunch of energy bars and lukewarm instant coffee, we were back in the canoe, happy with how agile it was unburdened from the packs. After a week of fishing open water structure, it felt good to be back in the shallows again, fishing shorelines and cover. Eventually we found ourselves where a medium-size creek poured into a protected bay. I could feel the spot's promise in my body and blood. There's just something magical about where moving water enters a lake.

We each caught fish on our first respective casts, and two hours later hadn't moved more than a hundred yards. There was no need; the bay was alive with pike. If by chance you managed to pull your offering back to the canoe without an eat, you'd scratch your head, twitch your fly or lure boatside to make sure it hadn't fouled, and in doing so raise a terrible thrashing that required a thorough cleaning of your sunglasses. The speed and ferocity of the pike were a shock to the system after the relatively genial assaults of lake trout and walleye. All fish are killers, of course, but the northern pike is something special, predation in its purest form. It is the perfect weapon, bow and arrow in a single package, ready to spear anything swimming by: a duckling, a bullfrog, a rabbit-strip streamer worked through the brightness of a boreal spring day. To understand the pike is to understand the ferocity that lives in all fish. In the pike, it just lives brighter.

For the next few hours we enjoyed fishing action that would have made our 10-year-old selves' jaws drop onto the plywood floor of our johnboat. The fish were not huge, only a few of them were even big, but they were strong and nasty, and we did not tire of their viciousness. And then we got a sign.

Jeff caught a midtwenties fish with a fleshy gash across the middle of its back through which a white curve of skull was showing. It didn't look like a spawning scar from another male, but rather that something very large had T-boned it. Sensing opportunity, we turned our attention to the deeper water just off the bay and started working a deep cabbage bed whose curling tobacco tips were just barely visible.

Nothing happened on the first pass, or the second. I tied on a heavier articulated fly and retrieved it so the white Schlappen tail feathers brushed the tips of the weeds five feet down, hanging up every now and again. On the third pass I let the fly drop through a gap in the weeds until it hung up on the bottom.

And then the bottom moved.

"Very big pike," I gritted. "Very big pike."

There are certain individuals of the species *Esox lucius* that have given the fish a bad name. If the pike is to return to a place of honor in the fishing pantheon, it will be because of specimens like this. No limp rag, this pike dug and raged, blitzed and charged. The last time a fish had put that kind of arc in my 10-weight had been a forty-five-inch muskie, and this, if it was possible, looked even thicker, its shape more barrel than snake. It was, I knew but dared not say, by far the biggest pike I had ever come into contact with, and I had lived a life of big pike. When it breached near the boat, I saw that the creamy white disks on its side were the size of grapes.

Knowing a pike of this size could not be lifted into a canoe without tipping it, Jeff steered the fight toward an island to land the fish. He steadied the canoe as I clambered out.

"Camera," I blurted.

My brother pulled out his point-and-shoot.

"No. Big camera. In the Pelican case."

I worked the fish as Jeff got the Nikon out. I could already see myself on the cover of a magazine. "Pike of the Year," the large block letters beneath me would read. My brother would get the photo credit. We'd go viral, become world-famous fishing brothers, and it would all begin with this fish. I just needed to land it. After one more push the fish came shallow and tipped its belly slightly upward in submission. Without a net, I grabbed the line just above the wire leader and pulled toward me.

We never touched.

It's hard to know the wild secret places energy is stored, where it comes from, where it goes. I'll never understand how that calm morning snatched our canoe, and I'll never understand how that gasping pike summoned enough energy to explode away from me. It could have swum through rock. The rod dove down and sprung back, the recoiling blank thwapping my forehead. My line was busted, the fly vanished, the fish lost. My best pike ever. Gone.

This is the part where, if you're a good angler and fishing partner, you stay quiet.

My brother did the one thing better.

"Just imagine what our childhood selves would say if they were here," he said.

In a perfect backcountry trip, one would find some way to rest before making the journey back. And on certain past trips, my brother and I had done just that, suffering greatly during the first half of the trip so as to create an easy last few days.

This was not that kind of trip.

After coffee the following morning, in front of our final fire, Jeff unrolled the map, colorless except for red dots connected by red lines. Each was a portage. And between us and our truck at the edge of the park were eighteen of them.

Eighteen.

"This is the last day we agreed on," Jeff said apologetically. "If nothing else, we'll remember this day."

I nodded. There would be no more babying my ankle. Unless I shouldered my share of the work, there was no way we'd get out of the park in time for Jeff to make his flight—the first of four flights, each plane bigger than the one before, that would take him from Red Lake, Ontario, to New York, New York.

We set out at first light, angling the canoe toward the wisps of yellow and pink stacked above the gray islands, and I wondered how the woodland caribou, those ghosts of the forests we never glimpsed, regarded our departure. The paddling was hard in the early going, not surprising given we'd both lost ten pounds and were likely eating ourselves by now, feeding on the fat we'd stored in that other, cushy life we'd left for a while but were now returning to. But I didn't feel any kind of excitement at the creature comforts awaiting us. If anything, I was filled with a sense of regret that we were going to let these wild shapes we had finally achieved go to waste. Eventually the paddling got easier. By late morning I felt as strong as I had all trip, ready to paddle for all eternity, to lose myself forever in a hazy blur of quiet strokes.

"Next time we'll need more Scotch," Jeff said.

"Yes. And more salt. We ran low on salt."

"But less gear. Next time no tripod," he said. "And maybe just one camera lens."

"We'll move slowly and deliberately. No accidents. All good decisions."

I knew it was too early to tell yet whether this was just fun-talk or something more serious. The decision to make another trip would come, if it did, during a time of deep quiet. During the dead of winter when you feel as trapped as your plowed-in car. In the middle of your fourth meeting of the day, your brain numbed beyond repair. Somewhere in that sterile interval, there may come a burst of life you didn't know you had, a surging energy when you thought there was none. And it will be in that moment of irrepressible vitality that you'll remember the feeling of open water made just for you, there once more, still there waiting, if you can only carry yourself to it.

CHAPTER 3

Mad Men

Each winter I go North for spring break. "Spring" in this case is late February, a solid month before the season's official launch. North means north of Ann Arbor, Michigan. I do so for the pleasure of spending the days up to my chest in freezing water, catching a weekly quantum of fish that can usually be tallied by a single, cold-clawed hand. In the Upper Midwestern calendar, late February means deep winter, and we are reined in by cold and snow: streets halved by snowbanks, cars cased in ice, eaves fanged with icicles so long and sharp you must break them with a broom to safely enter and exit your house. My students go as far south as time and their parents' money will allow, returning illicitly tanned, poachers of a foreign sun. My colleagues hole themselves up in their offices to catch up on grading and research.

I head north to swing flies.

Most often I go alone, though I've had a few joiners over the years. A friend—sometimes an angler, sometimes not—will get infected by my enthusiasm, the strange glow I start to emanate midwinter, and conscript themselves to the cause. But after spending a few days of subarctic swinging, these friends find themselves utterly perplexed. An entirely fishless, tugless day—and in a week of winter fishing there's always one, if not more—usually breaks their spirits, and they spend the rest of the trip creating excuses to stay indoors. So even those excursions that begin with the promise of companionship end with me crunching alone along the shelf ice, asking a question all serious anglers have asked themselves once if not many times, as they swish upstream after midnight in the wake of a hatch that never material-ized, or swing open the door of a top-secret PO Box to which small but expensive packages of tying materials arrive off the radar of a significant other. That question: Am I mad?

﹀

Then one fall a colleague put me in touch with a Russian PhD student named Ivan, an intensely obsessive angler and fly tier who, like me, often fished alone. A warmwater, bass-only guy, he had never caught anything of the Salmo order, was not familiar with the term "base layer," and had never mended a fly line in his life. But he jumped on board without a second thought, and two weeks later we crammed my car full of fur, food, and beer and struck out over the winter barrens of central Michigan, destined for white pines and the Lake Michigan tributaries on the western side of the state.

Ivan's introduction to winter steelheading began on a typical midwinter Michigan morning, with extreme cold singeing every exposed swatch of skin: fingertip, nose tip, nape of neck. I rowed hard for the first twenty minutes, both to get my blood moving and to reach a key confluence below which the river would be deeper, slower, and maybe a little warmer. The steelhead were in various states. While most sulked in ghostly torpor in the deepest, slowest runs, a fair number of early spawners were taking up position on gravel. They splintered off their redds as soon as the boat approached, cramming their oversize bodies into the blue slots above and below. There were, all in all, plenty of fish in the river—we had good fall rains and a few midwinter thaws to thank for that. Swinging sculpins, we averaged a nip or tug every few hours, and by day's end had each caught decent fish, mine a solid female with deep-red sides that had leapt like it wanted to shatter the sky.

"So," Ivan asked at the takeout, blowing heat onto his hands. "Do you think the fishing will pick up?"

His question caught me off guard.

"Actually," I said, "we did pretty damn good." I explained to him that we were pursuing wild steelhead in the dead of winter, and that each one of these fish was incalculably special. I told him about the steelheaders of the Pacific Northwest, who might fish for days or even weeks on end without even making contact with a fish. At that he stopped picking the ice off his bootlaces and gave me a very particular look. And so I added something I both didn't believe and didn't need to believe: "I've got a feeling tomorrow will be better."

—◦—

The next few days were more or less identical. We would put in at daybreak and take out at dusk, a span of about eight hours punctuated by a few rounds of coffee, smoked sausage, bread, and candy bars—and often, but not always, a fish. We paid close attention to our flies' appearance and movement in the water, taking mental notes on current speed, clarity, and drop rate and which patterns and colors garnered interest and which did not. Evenings found us back at our vises, forging into being the best streamers the conditions could ask for. I would nod off at the vise and shuffle off to bed mid-fly, then wake in the morning dark and palmer my way to wakefulness. I can't speak for Ivan, but this singularity of purpose was one of the reasons I loved winter steelheading. As Kafka (who would have made a great winter steelheader) once wrote, "The closed system is pure."

Then midway through our trip, conditions changed drastically—a warm front brought a thawing rain, and the river came up fast, surging hard and black and gumming at the banks. In the dirty, ripping water we had our first entirely tugless, fishless day—not even a trout between us. That evening Ivan did much less tying and much more drinking, and on the river the next day he showed clear signs of defection: skipping perfect holes to develop a better system for storing anchor line, passing up fishy runs to organize the fly boxes by winging material.

I was losing him.

I countered by pointing out those elements unique to the world of winter steelheading. How few other people there were on the river. How damn good you felt after spending all day in the cold. How hard the fish fought, despite the frigid water temperature, when you did manage to actually hook up. But Ivan simply nodded politely before announcing that he was going to jog in place on the bank "to prevent hypothermia," an idea I couldn't quite understand since my own blood flushed hot with each new hole, each promising run, each change of flies. And, when toward the end of the day I caught our best fish of the trip—a terrific buck that rewrote, for me at least, the entire day in a glowing, fishful light—he responded, not by grabbing his rod, but by asking whether he could be full-time rower, since it might delay his freezing to death. Drifting toward the takeout at dusk, I realized that once again I'd failed to make a convert.

﹌

The night before our last full day, a huge winter storm hit. Sleet turned to snow and didn't so much fall from the sky as fill it, fallingly. On the TV, the meteorologists threw themselves into the storm with an urgency and relish usually reserved for tornadoes. Here they'd get eighteen inches of snow. Here fourteen. Here twelve.

Then the thunder and lightning started.

"This does not happen in St. Petersburg," Ivan said, following a particularly hot flash of light, a particularly angry growl of thunder.

"We call it thundersnow," I said. "It doesn't happen here all that often either."

Snow was still falling into next morning, and even the heavy-duty pickups were spinning out on the wet sugar. Still in my long johns, I put on my boots and poked around behind the lodge to get a look at the transformed landscape, amazed at how much snow was crammed onto every available surface. Even the twiggiest branch of the tiniest alder held heapfuls; with their soft powder freight, they reminded me of August antlers, thick and velveteen. The thermostat read twelve.

It was a dream come true.

"You can't be fishing in this," Ivan said as I tore through my layering material. He was propped up in bed on his laptop, earbuds in, ringed by notebooks and notecards. *But this is it,* I wanted to tell him, *the day we suffered for. The reason we're here.* But I didn't say that, or anything else—I knew my credibility had expired sometime midweek, back in the middle of a frozen, fishless day. And so I just smiled and shrugged, tucked a hot thermos of coffee into my slingpack, opened the door, and gave myself happily over to bright-white steelhead oblivion.

Walking the quarter mile to the access, the world felt much larger. The unending whiteness seemed to fling the horizon back a hundred miles and stretch the world to a taut, glittering canvas. Two snowmobilers whizzed past me at a railroad crossing, and I watched them as they plumbed the wide lane between the white woods. I'm generally not a fan of those whiny machines, but today they made perfect sense. How else could one fathom this deep white world? How else could one determine whether its promise of endlessness were true?

At the river I tied on a weighted woolhead sculpin and got started. I was midway through a promising run when I heard an ear-splitting crack and watched in horror as a massive white pine split itself down the middle and fell across the river just fifteen yards downstream from me. I went ashore to bypass the tree and check out the damage up close. The trunk had broken on a diagonal, almost lengthwise, the newly exposed wood glistening like fresh cut ginger. Once-hibernating insects squirmed in the open air. And even as I stood there, thankful to have escaped injury or worse, I heard another splitting crack off to my right and watched a mushroom cloud of fresh powdered snow rise up above the tree line and swell outward in the gray sky. It appeared the weight of this snowfall was too much for the tallest, oldest trees.

Wading extra slowly, with one eye out for widowmakers and the other for the river bottom's many sharp drops, I discovered lies I never knew existed: secondary runs that I usually walked past after swinging through the obvious water; short, deep pockets where they did not belong; narrows slots and chutes half hidden by logjams. I was deep into my second pair of gloves when I felt a sharp, ripping tug—a hot fish. It fought with the strength of a fall specimen, peeling line and surging for a snaggy cutbank, and I was forced to push my tippet to the limit to keep him on. It worked. The fish braked, the tippet held, and a few short surges later I was backing the two of us up onto a shallow island of midstream gravel. I produced my forceps and removed the hook without exposing the buck's gills to the crystallizing cold, admiring it briefly, an upper twenties buck flush with the dark colors of his river residency. *Who was this strange, solitary creature?* I wondered. Was it counting the days to spring? Waiting, like so many anglers back in their warm homes, in anticipation of a more primary performance? Or did it, like me, find this winter kingdom a perfect place unto itself?

A few minutes after I released him, the clouds lifted for the first time that day, and through the dull white wall I saw a scrape of blue, then a pale apricot light in the treetops. I stopped for a midstream cup of coffee when, from the corner of my eye, I saw a large object missile out of the water and belly flop down—my fish. It had recuperated enough to shake its fist at me, the kind of angry, defiant gesture I have only ever seen in just-caught steelhead. It leapt once more, tossing sickles of light off its body, then splashed one final time—and the winter stillness rushed back in.

Some might have called it a day at this point, but high on the list of fishing skills I'll never master is the art of knowing when to quit. So I fished for another two hours, until my third and final pair of gloves soaked through and my reel only turned in stuttering rips of ice. Until I had to bring the rod to my mouth and nibble the river from the guides, crystal meat from steel bone. Until my neoprene waders grabbed my reel like Velcro, and my left hand went so numb I had to flex my biceps for a good while to get the blood back into my digits. When I finally started the walk back, my inner gauge told me I had just enough strength and flexibility to make it to the lodge.

"How was it?" Ivan asked when I stumbled back into the room, a frosted zombie too stiff to get out of his jacket.

What could I say? That, having caught one fish in the great snow palace, I'd had an absolutely perfect day on the water? That I had possessed my own little Xanadu of flow and frost, had caught the moment I'd been chasing all week? That in that dark water and winter fallout I on honey dew hath fed, and drunk the milk of Paradise? With winter steelheading, you either get it or you don't, and there's no amount of fancy language that's going to change that.

"One for one," I said, then hurried into the bathroom and thrust my cold hands under warm water and stood there, smiling, for a very long time.

CHAPTER 4

Cloud, Castle, Creek

With each new course we lose a hitchhiker. Tripe soup with marjoram petals sees a young man in a ratty tracksuit off into an orange Fiat. Schab Bosmański—aka "Bossman's Pork," a total eclipse of the pork by an even larger piece of pork—attends to the departure of a Slavic carnival-worker type, his whorled comb-over an errant star from a Van Gogh night. Now all that remains at the edge of the highway, just a few yards away from our table at this culinary annex of a rural gas station, is a tall, pretty blonde-haired girl with crème de menthe fingernails and a straw cowboy hat.

"Does the United States not have hitchhikers?" Arek asks through a mouthful of potatoes.

"These just seem more confident of not being murdered."

Arek smiles. His girlfriend, Aga, laughs. This roadside meal we're sharing, so fresh and good it should make any American road-tripper shrivel before their chicken potpie *taquito*, is at once a first date, a geography lesson, and a fishing consultation. Arek looks the part of a fly-fishing guide—he sports a freshly shaved head, thick-framed glasses, and a beard long enough to tuck into his T-shirt, like a hair cravat. But since getting picked up from the Wrocław train station an hour ago, I've learned two things that make me a little uneasy. For one, Arek doesn't drive—that's his girlfriend's purview. Secondly, and perhaps more dubiously, he's never caught a trout.

"Small problems," he says with a wave of the hand as our *stek tatar* and vodka arrives. He is, he assures me, a master coarse angler, and one whose position as urban fishing editor for Poland's most revered fly-fishing magazine means he knows every trout-fishing guide and lay fanatic in the country, even as he prefers chasing asp and zander in urban shipping canals. More important for me, an adjunct college writing instructor, his services are free—all that's required is a little collaboration with my words and his photos. And that is the kicker.

While I'd like to write that I've cashed out my savings account to pay for this trip, the fact is that I don't even have one, and even my checking account, by month's end, is usually one restaurant cheeseburger away from an overdraft fee. But my profession does afford me one key benefit, a boon better than money—four-month summer vacations that I spend chasing the bugs and sleeping in my tent, car, or friend-of-a-friend's fallow deer camp.

This lifestyle, I regularly explain to the well-adjusted people I meet, is not a hobby but a matter of survival. Away from rivers, strange maladies befall me. There pass weeks on end when I can't get a full breath. My ears start to ring with the sibilance of steak knives on dinner plates. My muscles start to twitch, imperceptibly at first, but by late February, when I have not fished in some time, my calf resembles the keyboard of a player piano. The remedy is always water. Up to my knees in a river with a fly rod in my hand, all spiritual and biological systems function keenly. And so my life revolves around getting as much angling time as possible, usually in the company of brown trout, a fish I admire so much I've decided to chase them in the part of the world where they originated—overdraft fees be damned.

"*Na zdrowie*," Arek says, raising his glass.

"*Na zdrowie*."

I drain the last of my vodka. Arek and Aga scoop up the last of their *tatar*. As we get up to settle the bill, I feel comfortably lower to the ground. The fields glow a richer gold. The sun burns softer in the sky.

"What about her?" I ask, pointing to the blonde hitchhiker, who hasn't yet been whisked away.

Arek smiles and shakes his head. "Firstly, there is no room. Doubly, she is desiring another direction."

It's true. In my more general disorientation I hadn't noticed that each of the hitchhikers had been queuing into the flow of traffic heading back toward Wrocław. Our lane, the one that will take us farther from the fields and cities and lead us deeper into the forests and mountains, has almost no traffic at all. And so I watch her shrink in the rearview, the lone skyscraper of Wrocław disappearing behind her shoulder, as we ourselves press west, through luminous fields of wheat and rye, past watercolor houses and medieval church spires, toward the wintergreen saddles of the Karkonosze Mountains.

The first time I traveled to Poland I was 11 years old. It was about a year and a half after Communism had fallen and my aunt, who my mother had not seen in fifteen years, was getting married. My brothers and I were taught no Polish growing up, but by the time we landed in Warsaw we could each repeat a token phrase. Mine was to be delivered to my 92-year-old blue-eyed great-grandmother: "My mother says I have your eyes." More useful would have been: "Please don't let us die." The trip nearly killed all of us in different ways. My brothers and I, children of the antiseptic suburbs of the antiseptic '80s, were not ready for milk sloshed straight from the cow or water cranked straight from the well; we spent most of the trip trying not to soil ourselves, then, when this proved impossible, trying not to soil ourselves when we had company. My father fell ill with a fever that peaked to 105 the night of the wedding and rendered him unable to defend himself from the groomsmen who pulled him from bed for vodka and dancing. One might think my mother would have enjoyed some sort of home-field advantage, but she in fact came closest to death, suffering a third-degree burn on her leg after mishandling a tub of boiling laundry water, then contracting hepatitis C from the single needle the local clinic used to treat everyone that came in that day.

Elevated above my memories of suffering are those of watching my uncle fish the oxbows of the Wisła River on calm evenings after the wedding festivities had ended. He was tall and tremendously mustached and, despite being thin as a rail, had hands so chronically swollen from farmwork he often broke his cigarettes as he pulled them from the pack. My mother had spoken of his fishing prowess for years, and as a result my fish-obsessed brothers and I regarded his every action with great reverence. While he purportedly had some actual rods stashed away somewhere, his preferred method of fishing was gillnetting, which he practiced from a homemade wooden boat that took on water just slowly enough to allow him a single out-and-back expedition. He would row out across the black water to lay his net, then back off and smoke a few cigarettes before pounding an oar violently on the surface of the water. The percussion sent any fish in the vicinity fleeing straight into his trap: pike, chubs, zander, carp. My brother and I would help carry the fish home—everything was kept, no matter the species or size—then watch our uncle cut off their heads and thumb out their guts and halo their bodies with loops of onion; or pack their cavities tight with marjoram, onions, and salt; or put them to sleep in the oven on a bed of red peppers and fresh cream. A subsistence angler through and through, he had no use for a fishing license, and had you given him something as inefficient for the taking of fish as a fly rod, he would have traded it for vodka and cigarettes. As such I can't help but wonder what he would think of me now, back in Poland twenty years later, about to spend quite a bit of money to get licensed to fly-fish just for fun.

"Fishing license." Driving past a coal plant toward what my American brain wants to call housing projects, I'm beginning to wonder if *license* is the right word. The documentation Arek has instructed me to bring along—Polish passport, American passport, notarized birth certificate, four black-and-white 2x2s that make me look like a young Stalin—suggests something a good deal more serious than the flimsy scrap of plastic that grants me access to any body of water in the state of Michigan. And because I'm still missing the final required document—proof of Polish address—we have to exploit a connection in the form of Aga's father's friend, who serves as president of a local fishing organization. And so my entrée into Polish fly fishing begins in a Soviet-era housing complex and the presidential chambers of the Lower Silesia Catfishing Club.

"Do you see the entrance?" Arek says after we circle the complex twice.

A whistle shrills from the back of a loading area, and out from between a dumpster and a stack of broken pallets emerges a bald, hulking individual who introduces himself as Ryszard. There's little presidential about him, unless you count his bandaged headwound as evidence of some poorly sized crown. He leads us to a dank bunker office lit by a single bulb hanging from an extension cord. There are bobbers in the pen holders, lead pyramid sinkers for paperweights, a klatch of spinning rods in the corner, old throw-nets oozing from the ceiling. The only things without immediate piscatorial application are a plate of browning sugar cubes and two life-size posters on either wall, one a calendar featuring a thoroughly siliconized brunette in a black bikini stating, "We are going farther," the other a heavily airbrushed Bruce Willis standing in a field of rye wearing a face no American would recognize—a soft smile like he's about to invite you in for homemade eclairs. He's in that field hawking a vodka named for the 16th-century Polish king who saved Europe from the Ottomans. The text at the bottom of the poster is in English, and I can't help but think that someone on the design team outsourced the translation to Google: "It's the best vodka I'm familiar with."

The already ruesome getting-legal process is further complicated by the fact that Ryszard has only ever processed licenses for what are referred to in Poland as "lowland rivers"—his is, after all, a catfishing club. Since high mountain streams, not to mention fly fishing itself, are subject to different laws that are completely foreign to him, we have to sit through endless phone calls, web searches, and consultations with dusty reference tomes. Stamps are needed from this Ziploc bag, holographic stickers from another. Nearly every page in one of the booklets I will have to carry requires the affirmation of a violently taloned Polish eagle, inked, blotted, and blown on with great care. Regular presidential cigarette breaks are required, and during one of these Ryszard asks, angler to angler, what it's like to catch a fish on a fly rod.

Being the only fly angler in a family of anglers, I have a lot of experience with this question, along with the suspicion that informs it. "It feels amazing," I reply, and offer to take him out sometime. He accedes, but insists we first go after the Wels catfish of the Oder River, punctuating the invitation by making a chopping motion against his thigh, like he's miming the amputation of his leg. It takes me a minute to understand what he's doing, but then I remember it's what my Polish grandfather used to do when talking about the pike he had caught. Whereas an American will hold his hands out in front of you to denote the size of a fish, a Pole shows you how far the fish would stretch up his leg if its tail were placed at his toe. To his offer I reply, "*Bardzo podoba mi się*"—I'd love to—and mean it, the Wels being one of the fantasy fish of my teenage years. I wonder how one would go about taking one on a fly.

Back on the road, we celebrate my newborn legality with beer—in Poland it's legal for anyone but the driver to drink themselves into any state of intoxication the situation requires. "Curl your lips over your teeth so they don't chip," Arek advises. After an hour we stop to pee near a bridge over a small stream flowing through potato fields. Arek explains that in the 1980s the streams of this region ran a different color every day of the week, depending on which chemical dye the Soviet textile factories were using. "Even this color," he says, lifting a few strands of Aga's fire-engine-red hair. Each waterway was an ecological dead zone entirely void of life—home to not a single aquatic insect, not a single fish.

"But look now," he says. In the soft dusk a mayfly hatch is underway, and the river seethes with the fleshy porpoises of feeding fish. "Grayling," Arek smiles. "The big one under that branch." As a result of various grassroots conservation initiatives, many of them advanced by the small population of fly anglers in the country, the rivers are slowly healing. There is even a twenty-year plan to restore a reproducing population of Atlantic salmon to Poland's rivers, fish that haven't seen their native spawning grounds in the mountainous south of the country in hundreds of years. Arek's eyes water a little as he tells me all this.

"You are here at the right time," he says.

The sight of sipping grayling stays with me as we drink more beer and gain on the darkening mountains. A crescent moon has cleared the treetops when we pull into the farmyard of Arek's uncle, a chronophobic bachelor who keeps geese. I fall asleep on an air mattress in a room with forty clocks. None tick in unison. All count down one thing: Tomorrow we fish.

The Midwestern angler knows with intimacy the native habitats of a number of fish: There's the alder tunnels and black-tea currents of a Northwoods brook trout stream, the rocky bays where football-shaped smallmouth eat crayfish like popcorn, the deep weed beds above which pike and muskies float like clouds on sunny days. But for the last five years it's been the brown trout, an immigrant newcomer, that I feel most drawn to. I've caught wild, naturalized specimens in Minnesota, Michigan, Wisconsin, and Wyoming, but I've never guided into my net a native *trutta morpha*, have never seen up close the liquid loam from which its genus sprung. This trip to the Karkonosze will change all that.

By the time dawn breaks, we're already switchbacking into the mountains, their slopes thick with conifers erasing into fog. Water's everywhere—ribbons of snowmelt carving through moss, bright freshets glittering on black cliff faces, arterial creeks churling here and there beneath the road—and the air is so damp I can feel it on my skin. After some time we turn onto a darker, tighter two-track, ride it bumpingly onward until it deltas into a wide valley surrounded by mountains so tight with trees they look like humps of green coral. This, Arek explains, is the edge of the historical Kingdom of Silesia, now Poland; on the other side of the peaks in the distance lies the historical Kingdom of Bohemia, now the Czech Republic. Somewhere in the forested distance the Izera delineates, as rivers often do, the border between worlds.

We disembark before a large structure of stacked stones that from one angle looks like a pile of glacial rubble, and from the other, a miniature castle. Arek explains it's the last surviving building of an old Prussian glassworks recently repurposed as a base camp for backcountry explorers—our digs for this fishing trip. We unload our gear and claim our beds amidst the snores of other campers. Dew glistens on the wreckage of the previous night's revelry: sardine tins, sausage nubs, smoked cheese, enough beer and Becherovka to disable a small army. From a thermos Aga pours us hot beet broth spiked with almost too much black pepper. We drink it defensively—the cold is going nowhere—before wadering up and heading off to find the Izera.

We hear the river before we see it. From a high forest bluff it appears as one long chute of broken water, lashing through bedrock, crashing between boulders, all ropes of foam and gyres of froth. As we begin our descent, slower stretches start to reveal themselves, and I get the old feeling, part trance, part twitch, that accompanies all my encounters with flowing water.

We spend the next hour less as anglers than mountain goats. Navigating from boulder to boulder over the roaring pocket water is tough, the fishing tougher. An hour in, I'm not seeing or catching anything. Neither are Arek or Aga, who take a break to forage up some lunch. Resorting to the old fly-fishing fallback of pure observation, I choose a piece of water and stare at it long enough to glimpse a riseform in the chaos, a hand-size trout snatching a size 20 caddis in a plot of calm the size of teacup. Kicking my peripherals into gear I start to see clipped shadows, dark flinches, little stabbings of life at the bases of boulders as I jump between them. Trout. None big, some not small. I switch to an ultra-buoyant dry fly and start dappling in whatever pockets of slack I can find. To get my fly to stay put in an eddy, I have to hold not only my fly line but the thick butt section of leader off the water. My fly hangs for one second, two, three, and then with a bloop disappears.

I steer my first native brown trout carefully through the boulder field, pushing my tippet to breaking each time it lunges beneath a boulder. When I scoop it up and lay the fish out on a patch of wet moss, it's a dark gold, almost black, a fish who spends most of its life hidden under rocks. I find a piece of slack water for the release, then retrieve my Moleskine to take some notes. My fishing friends will no doubt ask what it feels like to catch a native brown trout in the land of its forging, and I will need to have a good, precise answer. *I'm overcome*, I scribble, *by a feeling of being held together more resolutely in space, a barrel receiving its bands.*

I catch three more before rejoining Arek and Aga, who've returned with spoils: bright-red currants, dark wild blueberries, a heavy haul of fat boletes we'll cook in cream for dinner. Aga breaks one of the mushrooms in half for my benefit, shows me the flesh flush blue. After postprandial beers I lie back on a mossy slab of rock and, with the rich white noise of water surrounding me, lean back into a nap. Beside me Arek and Aga speak in low, intimate tones, and I recall the many times I've bedded down listening to one sound or the other, flowing water or the Polish language—in the childhood lullabies my mother would sing to me, in the joyful yelling mixed in with the joyful drinking that echoed up the stairs of our Southside Chicago home, in the midnight elocutions of the Kickapoo or Au Sable Rivers, flowing so close to my tent I'd dream of inundation. And I hear for the first time moments where the sounds of the water match perfectly with the sounds of the words—the *ś* of foam parsing cobble, the *sz* of an eddy curling into itself, the droning *ż* where heavy water grinds against a log, the bright *ć* of water splattering onto rock—and in something between a thought and a dream I imagine the birth of the Polish language as a small boy squatting beside a brook and mouthing the sounds the fleeing water gives him, I hear him calling after the water in the water's own voice.

⟋⟍⟋⟍

I wake sometime later. The light's canted, Arek and Aga are gone, but they've left a note—it reads "UPSTREAMS"—so I hike up and over into the next valley. Here the river has an entirely different character, no longer a roaring boulder field but a gently purring creature so slow I can make out the water's color: melted sugar just before it starts to burn. A cloud of yellow stoneflies hangs against the blue sky, their wings humming in a creamy blur, while below them trout rise with a lazy, dripping-faucet rhythm. I'm overcome with the feeling of being alone at the top of the world, and I can tell this is going to be one of those days when you remember not just the fishing but the in-between spaces, too, the shadows of clouds rippling over spruce, the nods of wildflowers as bees launch off, the sharp whiffs of juniper in the breeze.

My first cast is to a likely riffle, a pinch of two high banks where the river flows over cobble and makes a sound like a melting piano. When my fly bobbles over a submerged boulder, the water snaps shut on itself, and a brown trout pinballs frantically through the pool. It leaps once, a sickle of sunlight, and a few moments later I guide him onto a shoal of pebbles. This fish is brighter in color than his fast-water cousin, a pale gold trending to silver, with tiny red spots, like drops of wet blood.

With the next fish I catch I'm startled by a burst of clapping coming from the trees. It's not Arek or Aga but a family of hikers stopping by the river for a drink. A small boy among them picks his way out into the stream by way of dry stones. He looks like he wants nothing more than to enter the water, grab the rod, and learn to fish, and I'm reminded of how strange and magical fly fishing can appear, to pull perfect glittering confections of life from a few inches of crystal clear water where nothing could be seen but sand and cobble. How it seemed less like a fish had been living there, more like the river had simply pressed itself together into a shape of gold and silver, eaten the bug, fought the rod, and diffused into water again.

I play the next fish all the way to the boy's feet. He touches the tip of its nose with a finger and smiles deeply, not an everyday smile but the wide, teary-eyed grin of a child discovering some new enchantment. He looks almost like he wants to cry, and I wonder if this is the moment that will lead him on his own journey to water.

I unhook the fish and place it in a still pocket behind my boots, but it needs no rest, it's off and away with two flicks of its tail, splitting a pair of boulders as it angles upstream, making a little wake as it pushes through a riffle, then disappearing into a dark pool with a single large cloud reflected in its center, a white iris.

Just then Arek and Aga appear at the top of a hill, waving me toward them. I say goodbye to the family and rush to meet my friends.

"This is the most perfect creek I have ever fished," I tell Arek. "I want to fish it again. I want to fish it forever."

But he only puts his hands on my shoulders and points his rod upstream, beyond the green hills to the distant haze of the next valley, and smiles.

"We are going farther."

CHAPTER 5

Why I Do Muskie Camp

First things first: Muskie camps are not a thing. As far as I know, my friends and I run the only one in existence. I'm not even sure that *camp* is the right word. There's no wood plaque with a hand-carved rainbow trout that would welcome you to a fish camp, only a crush of reeds where we pull the boats up through the alders and out of sight. There's no shack with a woodstove and eight-pointer hanging on the porch, though we share the deer hunter's indifference to hygiene. No, our muskie retreat is a tent-and-tarp, public-land sort of affair, our only residential luxury the waxed canvas A-frame our spiritual leader, an enthusiast of 18th-century voyageur culture, packs along from time to time. By day, we ply the black water for muskies. By night, we drink whiskey under a dark sky. Sometimes, but not always, we smell like *Esox*.

Explaining how our first camp came about is simple: We plotted the farthest-most point from any paved road in the Midwest and went to check the fishing. The river we settled on, a swampy, low-country watershed that defied development and swallowed two tracks whole, was so little known we dared not bring anything but a canoe. That first year we paddled a full ten miles looking for high ground to camp on and eventually found it, along with a wolf pack that howled to either warn or welcome us, no one can say which. And we caught fish; or rather, one of us caught enough fish to make the others believe they could too.

Explaining how muskie camp happened for the first time is one thing. But accounting for why it stuck, why muskie camp became an annual event with all the fixity of Christmas—explaining that is another thing altogether. If I had to come up with a reason—and my editor deems this wise—I'd hazard it's for the particularly sublime nature of the discoveries made at muskie camp. These are not your everyday bits of knowledge. They have little to no application to the outside world. They won't make you money or find you love, can't help you out with a flooded basement or do your taxes. And yet—or maybe because of this—the teachings of muskie camp seem to be essential lessons for the good life, or at least the life I care to live.

Because of muskie camp I can think through the origins of faith and its variations, since any muskie fly box is an attempted conversation with the Unknown.

Because of muskie camp I know that the shape of a river also has a sound, best played by the stylus of an old Evinrude, best heard over the crackle of a campfire.

Because of muskie camp I know that whiskey has utilities beyond the mere tonic, that on moonless nights it becomes an agent of navigation, conferring if not sight itself then at least the conviction of it, which is sometimes superior.

Because of muskie camp I know that a man who makes a terrible housekeeper when surrounded by brooms and vacuums can become, when handed an axe, the dictionary definition of neatness. That black bear backstrap is first and foremost a breakfast food, especially when wrapped in venison bacon.

Because of muskie camp I know if you get lucky once, you revel, and if you get lucky twice, you row. That the human body is a tool whose edges fade with time, though there are activities that provide fair compensation for the blunting.

Lastly, I now know that not all time is created equal—that muskie time, those rare minutes spent in hand-to-hand combat with a fish, is exceptional. Though few in number (spread out over a lifetime, even the luckiest in our group will be hard-pressed to break the ten-minute mark by the time he makes his Final Cast), these moments are great in size, towering over all those hours caught in traffic, blotting out years spent staring at screens. And they keep growing in height, those muskie memories, year after year. Maybe, in the end, that's what makes muskie camp so special, the great size of your life there when you look back on it—so tall you can barely, even on a clear day, see the top.

CHAPTER 6

In Patagonia

THERE ARE TWO WAYS TO GET TO PATAGONIA—PISCATORALLY speaking. The first and most foolproof method requires considerable foresight. You spend your youth cultivating employable skills, study something respectable in college, get a decent job, save your money. If you are truly clever, you don't even take up fly fishing until right before your trip, so as not to spend decades leeching the very cash you'll need for the expedition. (Harry Middleton once characterized fly fishing as standing in a bucket of ice water casting hundred-dollar bills into a fire, and I have not found this to be untrue.)

The second way is more fun, provided you don't mind your fly rods doubling as 401K and living without a permanent mailing address. It's also a total crapshoot. You study poetry in college, then spend your young adulthood fishing your brains out for an irresponsible interval, bartering words to offset your fishing costs and hoping that one day the red phone under the glass dome will ring and summon you to New Zealand or Kamchatka or some other such place you'd otherwise need to hawk an organ to afford. This is more or less how I found myself on a midnight flight over South America, watching the golden lights of Rio de Janeiro twinkle in the darkness and trying to access the part of my brain where my high school Spanish was sequestered. By the time I made my final landing, two planes later in the small Argentine town of Esquel, I had unearthed a single sentence: *"Hoy es mi cumpleanos."*

At the airport I met the driver who was to take me the rest of the way, three hours over the Andes into lush, wet Chile, or Green Patagonia, as he called it. But first there was lodge resupply work to be done. Had I been a traditional client I might have found going from shop to shop carrying crates of cheese and cases of beer a little dubious, but this was my first time dipping my toe into the travel bar-ter economy, and if there was work to be done in addition to fishing and writing, I was darn happy to do it. And so it was that my first glimpses of Patagonia came from behind a wooden crate of Johnny Walker Blue Label balanced on my lap. I saw great green mountains fluted with snow, gaping valleys with their spring crush of wildflowers, and molten blue rivers in precipitous canyons. I got a feeling—a spiritual awakening, if you will—akin to the time I saw true wilderness for the first time in the form of Ontario's Boundary Waters Canoe Area. For a Southside Chicago kid who'd been getting by on pinner bullhead in heavily nitrated municipal ponds, that foray north had been a life-altering trip. Staring out at the scroll of blue glaciers and misty rainforest, I wondered what sort of existential havoc Patagonia would wreak.

It was dusk when we pulled up to the lodge on Lago Yelcho, a shimmering mirror of purple twilight cradled by smoky mountains. The lodge manager showed me to my room and gave me the rundown of the next ten days. Breakfast at eight, lunch at the lodge or on the lake, my call, dinner from dusk until ten. Open bar with everything from espresso to whiskey available at all times; just sidle up and grunt. ("Only not the Blue Label," he clarified. "That is for the owner when he visits.") I unpacked, ordered up a Jack and Coke, walked the beach, and stuck my nose out into the night air. We Midwesterners can sniff the snow and tell you how deep it is, but we lack the mountain-born aptitude of apprehending space. How far off were the mountains on the other side of the lake? Hundreds of yards? Dozens of miles? The smell of perfectly scorched lamb coming from the beach hut broached more pressing questions—Carménère or Malbec?—and I was ready, after thirty hours of travel, to entertain some answers.

❧

The next morning I needed two servings of crisp bacon to un-gob the lamb from my gums. I followed this with eggs and apple pie, did a sign of the cross for my cholesterol, then went down to the dock to wait for the head guide, Nancho, my fishing partner for the next ten days. Of the three boats bobbing in the surf, two were newer fiberglass models, the other a battle-scarred aluminum semi-V with a homemade plywood casting deck, hand-carved oars, and a 20-horse Evinrude. I prayed that this would be my boat. If I was going to fly to the other side of the Earth to throw feathers at trout, I wanted as much mojo as possible. When Nancho appeared on the dock he was crab-walking a heavy boulder wrapped with rope, and it took me a moment to realize that this was the anchor. He grunted a smile as he shuffled past the two new skiffs and plopped the great stone smack into the bottom of my dreamboat. We shook hands. I was thrilled. Any more mojo and we might not float.

I liked Nancho immediately. He was like a brother in the sense that you could fish without talking for an entire day and still be in constant meaningful communication. We spoke rarely, and only in four-word spurts. "Cast to the chore," he'd say in English, making a chopping motion with his hand. "Today is my birthday," I'd respond in Spanish. And we would both laugh.

My editor and the lodge manager had agreed on a general strategy to show off the diversity of the local fishing program there. Our first agenda item was exploring the dragonfly fishery, one of the primary draws of the Los Lagos region and Yelcho Lake in particular. The basic premise was that if you had sun, you had dragonflies—but also wind. Thus the art of dragonfly fishing consisted of seeking out wind-protected coves and keeping the boat right on the seam such that your backcast was battered by turbulence and your forward cast unfurled through calm air. You'd stand patiently on the bow watching pairs of dragonflies in complex mating maneuvers until suddenly, out of nowhere, a twenty-inch brown or rainbow built like an NCAA football would launch from the reeds, chomp at the bug, and crash back down. Sometimes the fish hit their mark, sometimes they knocked the bug to the water and spun back to eat it, and sometimes they missed entirely. The key to successful dragonfly fishing was to put your fly down where the fish landed, not where it launched. I spent the next two days with my 6-weight bent at angles I'd only seen at the end of rod-factory tours—the part where they give everyone safety glasses, let fly some engineer talk, and shatter a few blanks. I found myself with new appreciation for all those numbers and diagrams. *This*—I thought as I winched up one fish after another, *this is why math was invented.*

Next on the agenda was hitting the rivers with the big rods. I was particularly excited to do some streamer fishing, hailing as I do from one of the premier vortices of streamer intelligence—Southeast Michigan. It's where the Northern Michigan trout streamers of Galloup-Madden lineage cross-pollinate with New Age synthetics of Ohio's Steelhead Alley and get cooked in a cauldron stirred by the resident smallmouth and muskie freaks. As such I had a yellow plastic briefcase full of flies that moved like sclerotic eels on PCP, and I was eager to put them to work.

From my very first cast on the Yelcho River—fast and wide and blue and deep, with fortresses of sunken timber and white frothy rapids thick as cake frosting—I was smitten. The water, whose color I placed somewhere between Lucent Aquamarine and Crystal Blue, was basically a high-definition echo chamber for light. Your streamer itself flashed like a small rainbow, a small rainbow flashed like a steelhead, and a big chrome fish crashing in to eat was a detonation of silver stretching from here to there.

The clarity of the water and density of the fish meant I got to add a few new entries to my ever-growing taxonomy of trout eats. There was the homicidal lumberjack (a huge brown rolling out of a nasty logjam), the double puppy (two big browns wagging out from a cutbank like young mastiffs, fighting each other for the fly), and my new favorite, the busted compass (a rainbow spasming to locate a streamer just pulled from the water, then cracking it the moment it plops back down). Had it not been for the sedative quality of Carménère and red meat in pharmaceutical doses, I might have choked on my own adrenaline.

One evening at dinner I was debating whether to cancel all or only part of my previous life when the lodge manager put his hand on my shoulder and dealt me some horrifying news.

"We have a large party coming from Santiago at the last minute," he said. "We need all the rooms and boats. I am very sorry."

"What about a tent?" I asked.

"We will be using all the rooms, all the boats, *and* all the tents."

I was devastated. The weather the next few days was perfect for dragonflies, which is probably why the anglers were coming. At the same time, I understood that my hosts hadn't planned on this. And swapping out twenty paying guests for a single freeloading writer made clear financial sense.

"Don't worry, we will find you another place to stay," he promised.

I was packing my half-damp belongings when he returned twenty minutes later, smiling widely in the doorway and snapping a brochure in the air. "We have found you accommodations for the weekend. The owner is a friend of our owner. Our driver will drop you off this evening and bring you back Monday morning. There is no fishing but it is a very beautiful and unique place."

He handed me a brochure for a lodge that looked like it had been built by Frank Lloyd Wright's goofier cousin. Wedged into the side of a cliff overlooking Middle of Nowhere, Patagonia, it boasted its own farm, ranch, apiary, and orchards. I turned the page and saw a smiling man in a chef's hat cradling a plump Patagonian piglet with long brown fur. Above him the text read: "Unimaginable luxury in unimaginable surroundings."

"Full board?" I asked.

"Full board," he replied.

I nodded and stuffed the brochure in my pocket.

"I guess I have no choice."

That afternoon we rode the old skeletal horse of a Nissan three full hours, whether north or south or east or west I couldn't say. The last leg was straight uphill over shifting gravel, such a vertical driveway I wondered if they hadn't air-dropped this hotel into place. But when we finally flattened out at the top of the mountain, there it was, a magnificent structure, all polished wood and gleaming glass with nothing but the empty valley beyond. Shaking hands with the manager, a well-coiffed hotelier with French cufflinks fresh in from Madrid, I felt a little self-conscious about my wardrobe. My long-sleeve T-shirt was still damp from its sink washing, which had removed the trout slime but not the wine stains. There was also a nice loop of blood that had spurted from my head during a Malbec-induced casting accident, but this was only visible from behind. If I could keep the manager in front of me, like he was a tiger, I might keep my dignity intact.

I quickly learned that I was the only guest at the lodge, which in its grandiosity seemed more like a billionaire's pet project than something that would ever make money. As we walked the grounds, staff in headsets following close behind, I did my best to act like I had been in this kind of digs before, clasping my hands behind my back and muttering, "Very good, very good," at each and every opportunity. Eventually I was deposited in my bedroom, which had twenty-foot bay windows with remote-controlled wood blinds and a private balcony with a hot tub. I fired it up, hopped in, and wolfed down all the wine and chocolate in the welcome basket. "This might just redeem the indignity of not fishing," I thought.

For my afternoon entertainment I rode a brand-new mountain bike through empty foothills, twice parting a flock of lambs Charlton Heston style, then did a wet-dry-wet sauna sequence at the spa before heading to the dining room, where I was the only person seated among twenty white-linened tables. Dinner was a ten-course degustation anchored by sautéed squid in lavender oil, braised lamb with fig and Malbec reduction, and pork tenderloin with capers and Marcona almonds—followed by a Rube Goldberg–esque contraption of chocolate mousse, sculpted caramel, jellied fruit, and candied wildflowers. The way the head chef approached my table after my last bite—smiling and with an unbidden glass of Tokaj—made me suspect my host at the fishing lodge had told them I wrote for the *Wall Street Journal* and not a modest fishing magazine whose sum total of readers could have easily fit into a minor league baseball stadium. I thanked him for the meal, then repaired to the infinity pool to watch the sunset wick off the mountains. No sooner had I finished the Tokaj than the manager appeared and asked me a ridiculous question.

"Is everything to your satisfaction?"

Were this a movie, now would be the part where we flash back to the protagonist's rental in Michigan, complete with twin bed on the floor, tiny particleboard desk and plastic bins of fly-tying material stacked to the ceiling. It's a drizzly November evening, and the camera pans to our hero standing in the rain eating the tinned sardines his housemates have unanimously banned from indoor consumption.

But this isn't a movie.

"Very good so far," I said, handing over the empty wine glass and breaststroking to the middle of the pool. "Got any Blue Label?"

Word count constraints require that further details of my time at the palace of luxury must go unreported. Suffice it to say that when I returned to Yelcho Lake Monday morning I was a good deal more relaxed than the lodge staff, who had been put through the ringer by the party from Santiago. With no other reservations for the next two days, the lodge manager declared Monday a day of rest, and the grounds were relatively quiet. I was planning on a day of solo fishing from the beach when one of the younger guides, Ronny, knocked on my door. "Guides' day off," he said, smiling. "We go fishing. You too."

Late morning found Ronny, Nancho, and I careening down the Austral Road, a gravel highway connecting the north end of Chilean Patagonia to the south, blasting Creedence Clearwater Revival, of all things (*Greatest Hits*, volume 2). I was as excited as I'd been all trip. I knew that the water guides save for themselves is something special. It might be more beautiful, more remote, or more technical than client water. Whatever the case, the fish are usually bigger. Driving through a chain of Patagonia whiteouts, which is what happens when a semi-truck full of lumber passes you in the opposite direction (no one can see, no one slows down, it's as horrifying as it sounds), the only clue I had as to our destination were three bottles of wine in a fancy wicker basket. Someone was getting a bribe.

Eventually we turned off the main road onto a ranch, nearly hitting a goat, then a sheep, then a goat again. Every other mile or so Ronny would get out to open and close a gate. At times there was a two-track to follow, but more often than not the truck cropped pristine pasture. "Who else fishes this river?" I asked Ronny as Nancho got out to chat with the rancher, a heavily mustachioed fellow who ran with a gang of oxen.

He smiled. "Only us."

This river, which I am forbidden from naming, had an entirely different character from the other Los Lagos rivers I had seen. It was smaller, for one, and shallower, with triple the deadfalls of the bigger water. At its worst—which is to say, at its brown trout best—it was really just one long beaver dam with some flow down the middle, a channel of turquoise water riffling over cream-colored egg-size stones.

What followed was perhaps the single most magical fishing day of my medium-length life. Eighteen- to twenty-two-inch fish happened so often you took them for granted. Bigger fish came in spurts. In one half-hour window we netted twenty-four-, twenty-five-, twenty-six-, and twenty-seven-inch fish, all browns. The last and biggest, coming just before dark on a black articulated streamer, had launched itself airborne so spectacularly that I learned something new about the human tongue: *Whoa* is the same in every language.

As we motored back to the put-in at day's end, I was fully aware that I had beheld the promise of water fulfilled. You heard stories about it and maybe caught glimpses of it from time to time, but you never expected to find yourself there, flush against the dragon you'd been chasing since you could remember. What happens when you've held its tail in your hands? Do you put down the rod and take up something else? Master the game of horseshoes? Become an artisanal cheesemaker?

In my case, it led to me bribing Nancho to bribe the landowner to let us play with the dragons again. And we did, for three long, wonderful days that offered a better template for the afterlife than anything I had encountered in Catholic grade school.

And then, just like that, my time in paradise was done.

It was time, I supposed. I had gained twelve pounds, filled two notebooks, taken several thousand photos. My liver had pushed its dominion as far south as my kneecaps, and I had two slow-healing puncture wounds in my skull. Most surprisingly, I found myself pretty well sated fish-wise for the first time in my life. (If you don't know the feeling, it's a little like getting gassed at the dentist.) On the day of my departure I woke extra early, packed, wheeled my luggage into the lobby, and sat down to one final breakfast. The trip was over, and I was fine with that.

"Going somewhere?" the lodge manager asked me.

"Yes," I said. "Home."

His face froze for a moment before relaxing into a smile.

"You are joking, of course," he said, returning to his paperwork.

"No. I fly out this afternoon. Like we discussed."

I showed him the printout with my flight details. The color drained from his face.

"My God," he said. "I thought we had one more week. Tell me, did you fish the lagoons?"

I shook my head.

"Chase chinook with a single-handed rod?"

"Nope."

"Please tell me you fished tiny mayflies in the eddies?"

"I did not."

This last omission was apparently a deal breaker, because a minute later I was being shoved out the door with a mouthful of bacon and my 5-weight. It was, let it be noted for the record, one of three times in my life that I didn't feel like fishing. Nancho wasn't any more eager. Limping down from the guides' cabin with the lodge manager barking in his ear, he looked like a man who had not planned on being awake that day, and possibly the next. Time was of the essence, so we took a short cut across the very center of the lake, bouncing so hard over whitecaps I felt my vertebrae crumbling like shortbread.

"One hour," Nancho said when we arrived at our destination, a stretch of huge eddies over water so deep I could not see the bottom. When I got up on the casting deck, I saw beautiful rainbows picking mayfly emergers from the shifting scumlines. Nancho reached into the cooler and brought out not one but two beers. He uncapped them both, handed me one, and we clinked. I hadn't seen him drink all trip. Perhaps he hadn't needed to until now.

I flubbed the first few casts, then broke off a good fish when it dive-bombed a sprawling complex of timber some forty feet straight down. The break had happened midway up the leader; it would have to be rebuilt. I shook my head and took a swig of beer. My shoulder was pretty sore, my fingers cut up, my ears and cheeks scaly with sunburn.

"Forty-five minutes!" Nancho yelled.

I looked deep inside myself for room for these last fish, but the truth was I felt full to bursting. I'd just had ten days of the best fishing of my life, and there just wasn't any more space. Did I need to catch these fish to write about them? Couldn't I just have a beer and enjoy the scenery, like a normal person?

Then, from out of a cloudless, bluebird sky, there came a loud rumbling of thunder. I scanned the horizon. Nothing but sunshine.

Then it happened again, louder this time.

"Avalanche," Nancho said, pointing high into the mountains where rivers of snow were spouting off of cliffs and ledges, winter snowpack birthing new water. It made sense. Today was December 21st, after all, the first day of summer.

Then a voice in my head growled: *Don't you mean the first day of winter?*

Lord have mercy, I thought. In the long parade of sun and food and wine and fish I had lost sight of the fact that I lived in Michigan, where we'd be dogsledding to work for months and where there'd be no decent trout fishing till May. The realization cleared me out like a good belch.

"Thirty minutes!" Nancho yelled, but it wasn't just Nancho. It was Patagonia itself bellowing last and final call.

Slowly but deliberately, I got back up on the casting deck and took a deep breath. A pair of chrome cruisers entered my vector. Followed by a third. And a fourth.

Then I stripped out a ream of line. I singled out my target. I got ready to chug.

CHAPTER 7

Anglers on a Train

I. All Aboard

"Is it Sha-*ploo*?" Dan asks, making a sound like a heavy stone plopped in a pond.

"I think the guy at the gas station said *Chap*-low," Tom says. "Like Chapstick."

"Pretty sure it's Shap-*lee-oh*," Brian counters, going full French on it with a third syllable.

However you want to say it, it has taken the four of us almost two full days driving to get to the Northern Ontario town of Chapleau, a journey that saw more moose than bear and more bear than gas stations—exactly the ratio you're hoping for on a trip like this. The plan, as hashed out over a long winter's secret Facebook group, is to go lodge-hopping across the region by train and fish hard at each stop: pike and walleye at Lake Esnagi; pike, walleye, and brook trout at Lake Wabatongushi. I've driven solo from Ann Arbor, while Tom, Dan, and Brian have traveled together from Minneapolis. While I've fished with Tom a thousand times, the other two guys are new to me. In certain situations I'd have some trepidation about going deep in country with an untested crew, but Dan is Tom's brother, and I've come to believe that anyone with the Hazelton last name is piscatorially legit. And Brian Bergeson is one of those anglers whose name precedes him. A well-known fly designer and tier, his creations are responsible for hundreds of huge fish all over the world. As we stand around waiting for our locomotive to arrive, Brian opens his rod case to show off a custom 9-weight one of his globe-trotting clients recently gifted him for his role in taking a line-class record taimen. He winks as he resheaths the stick. "My flies don't mess around."

I crack open a nondescript Canadian pilsner and look out over the train platform, past clumps of men with their gear piled high into mountains, past a group of paddlers with two canoes bound for the

69

freight car, past a large contingent from Detroit with matching ball caps and bug nets—even though it's only late May and we are still pre-blackfly. There, beyond the curve of track, is our shared destination: the unpaved, ungridded country of the Canadian Shield. It's the first time I've approached hinterland this way. I've been dumped off on fishing trips from pretty much every other conceivable form of transport—by float plane, car, truck, four-wheeler, horse, kayak, and canoe. I once even did thirty miles of logging road on a mountain bike behind a wolf pack I took great pains not to gain on. But never, ever, have I taken a train.

This trainlessness is a shame given the importance of rail lines in shaping the modern sporting imagination. The first Canadian rail lines followed directly in the footsteps of the fur trade, connecting rivers like the St. Lawrence and Richelieu and essentially functioning as high-speed portages. They then expanded west with the timber industry, pushing the frontier farther year by year. And when the great harvest industries petered out, these same trains freighted sportsmen to the end of their respective lines, an era that coincided with the first outdoor magazines and the dreams they stoked: of remoteness, solitude, a quality of hunting and fishing unavailable in the backyards of civilization.

No other form of transport smacks as clearly of destiny as the train. Bush planes can change course and destination at leisure. Trucks and jeeps can do more or less as they please. But trains have a sense of fat-edness about them, and none more so than this particular line, which travels in only one direction per day. Today it's west through outposts like Larchwood, Ramsey, Missanabie, and Woman River; tomorrow east toward Esher, Azilda, Nemegos, and finally Sudbury. In a modern life that pulls you in so many directions you fear quartering on the regular, there's a deep comfort in the idea of a one-direction ride.

Finally the train pulls up and there's a bum rush to throw gear into the freight car. Even after the canoes and cases of beer, it's still only marginally full. I ask the conductor how far off Lake Esnagi is.

"Little under three hours, as the train flies."

II. LAKE ESNAGI

It's rare, in the boreal north, for spring to show the type of clemency for which it's elsewhere reputed. Here it's less of a season than a struggle, with most days striving hard in the direction of either winter or summer and generally achieving the goal by noon. Our arrival at Lake Esnagi coincides with an extended stretch of cold weather that has the walleye and brook trout fishing a little behind schedule. The pike, on other hand, are in full flush. We ask the head guide, Brent, which bay is best. "Pick one," is his reply.

Under low clouds we explore long, narrow bays fingering out from the main lake and the countless tributaries that seep into them. Pike with fresh spawning scars are recuperating in the vicinity of these out-flows, and we fish them all in a slow circuit, catching smaller fish first and then, as pike fishing goes, feeling our way out to larger specimens. The biggest females are hanging back on the edge of the deeper drop-offs, having finished their procreative business and wanting nothing more to do with the bumptious males. To my knowledge no one has yet assembled a complete compendium of pike eats, but by the end of the first day we have catalogued several dozen, from slow stalks to sudden razorings to the toothy arches of airborne *Esox*. A violent day of pike fishing recalibrates the angler's nervous system to a generalized expectation of ambush. Dark closets, blind corners, and even lidded toilets are afterward approached with extreme caution.

The next day we go walleye jigging with Brent, who totes along a massive cast-iron pan that looks like it could drop a bull moose. There's also a sack of potatoes and onions and a few cans of pork and beans. To this we'll add enough fish for a shore lunch, a great ritual of the North and the high tea of the angling class. Everyone who fishes the shield participates. Even diehard catch-and-release anglers understand that they are far enough from everyday life that the constraints of civilization do not apply. And it's a good thing, since in all the world you could not find a landscape better suited to shore lunch than Northern Ontario. Labrador is too thick with sphagnum and spruce, Alaska often too marshy and alluvial, but the Ontario shield is perfect and provides everything you need: an endless supply of dry wood, plenty of glacial rubble for architecting whatever fashion of stone stove you require, and islands that are just the right size—big enough to stretch your legs and explore, but small enough that you'll never need a search party.

I admit to not having jigged for walleye for several years, having been nursing a surface-fishing habit. I'd forgotten the sweet anticipation that builds with each lift and fall of the jig as you thump it down a bottom contour—*any second, any second, any second.* And then there's the electric tap-tap of the eat. Much has been made of the steelhead's take to a swung fly, or the toilet-bowl whoosh by which a bass Houdinis a hair-bug, but the take of a walleye directly beneath the boat has a primal poetry all its own, with your rod serving not only as a hook-setting tool but primitive scale. How heavy is this one? A good eater? Or even too big for lunch?

At high noon we go ashore with a few eater walleye and one smaller pike for variety's sake. Chef Brent goes to work, or tries to. Patience is not one of the virtues available to the angler who has fished hard all day in the open spray of a North country lake during what feels like late winter. And so we prowl around the fire like the fish we've been hunting, getting in his way and snatching up morsels whenever we can. Brent's potatoes are otherworldly, coming off his mandolin so thin you can see through them, then lolling in oil until they are crispy-burnt at the edges and gooey-soft in the middle. The final piece of the puzzle is the pork and beans. If you're new to the art of the shore lunch, the trick is to regard these not as a side dish but as a condiment, one that improves the taste of everything it comes into contact with. Along with hungry walleye and rapacious pike, Brent's five-star lunches become a part of our daily cadence, and by the end of our stay we have eaten and napped on four of the lake's dozen or so islands. But then it's time to move on.

III. LAKE WABATONGUSHI

Lucky are they who, already slaked from several days' good fishing, find themselves waiting in the woods for a train that will deliver them to many more. Our next stop is Lake Wabatongushi, which lays on the threshold of that country the early fur traders called Le Petite Nord, a continental divide of sorts that steers the rivers not south to Lake Superior but north toward Hudson Bay. Over a lunch of pork chops and cherry pie, a group of departing anglers tells us about the largest pike they'd ever seen in one of the bays, a fish that had closely inspected everyone's spoons and spinners but committed to none. Ryan, the head guide at the lodge, confirms the story and lays a map of the lake on the table. Holding a pen like an icepick in a heavily bandaged hand—dock-repair injuries are an Ontario rite of spring—he makes a few scratches on a small bay in the northwest corner of the lake. At first glance it looks like the jagged scrawl of a lie detector test, but when I rotate the map I see he's written the simple, honest word *BIG*.

All fishing trips have their own unique reflective interludes. Sometimes it's a long paddle or portage, other times an endless hike through the thick brambles of a mountain valley, or in those parts of the world where the heat is severe enough to gum up the hands of your watch, a lemonade siesta in the shade. But on the big lakes of Ontario, your dreamy reveries come in the form of ten-mile boat rides between islands of jack pine and great looming promontories of Precambrian rock. Cruising on the big open water of Wabatongushi on our way to see BIG, we see our first sunlight in days, great puddles of golden light that glide alongside the boat like manta rays before dissolving again into winter gloom. But this sun shower is a one-and-done. By the time we arrive at BIG's bay, it's as cold as it's been all week. In the early dusk a few snowflakes swirl about like midges.

There's a fundamental difference in approach between casting around a bay at random and targeting a known fish. Every action becomes more deliberate, starting with choosing your fly. I open my pike box and pour over the mess of feathers and flash. Selecting the correct size is easy—for a fish named BIG only the biggest will do—but there is color and profile to consider. I decide to heed the wisdom of the late Gary LaFontaine, a brilliant and eccentric fly tier who in some of his dry fly patterns advocated for matching not the colors of the natural bug but the tones of the prevailing light, which in this case means a steely blue suffused with magenta. I finally settle on a Murdich Minnow I tied years ago to imitate my brother's Purple-descent Rapala—a fish slayer if there ever was one. I give it a few twitches boatside to check out its colors. If an icicle and a baitfish had a love child, this would be it.

Tom and Dan start at one side of the bay, while Brian and I take the other. The idea is to work the shoreline inward and meet in the middle. Twenty minutes pass uneventfully, which is good because it suggests that smaller fish, sensing a dangerous appetite, have vacated the area—pike being cannibals and whatnot. Then, without warning, it happens.

There's a moment unique to pike and muskie fishing, the sudden heave of water when a fish of ample proportions pushes through the shallows after your fly. You know something is coming, and you know that the something is big. What's unclear, at least to a certain vestigial reptile part of the brain, is whether the toothy beast is coming after your fly or you. In this case it happens on my second cast to a grassy peninsula where the shallow water quickly drops to deep. "Big!" I yell as I set the hook again and again, not giving an inch as the fish digs and rolls. It tapes out at forty-two inches, the biggest pike I have ever landed, though not the biggest I've hooked. Returning to the lodge, I'm met with all the fanfare of a dragon slayer, beginning with beer and culminating in a trip to the bait house where, with a nub of chalk, I add my name and date to the lodge's fishing hall of fame.

Thus do we pass several blissful days of walleye afternoons, pike evenings, and cold woodstove nights. We have largely accepted by this point that our gamble to fish the first warm-weather pattern of the year has failed and the trip will end without chasing the local brook trout, who need a jolt to get them out of their winter torpor in the cold pothole lakes they inhabit. Then, on our last full day, we wake to enough heat that our first sentient thought doesn't involve fire. A quick step outside onto the deck confirms that the cold spell has broken at last. Today will be high sun and blackflies—and, we hope and pray, brook trout. At breakfast Ryan maps out a small lake deep in the woods that is full of nothing but char, and during our hike out we find the year's first morels, which we cram into all available pockets. At the lake there's an old johnboat hibernating in the grass, which we flip over and push into the shimmering blue bay. The lake is not large, but it is also not easy to read, and for the first half hour we twitch dry flies over shallow structure to no avail.

Then we start to get our eyes. Past the oars, just beyond the visible, the shadows of brook trout dart about in the depths, chasing baitfish. We go to sinking lines and weighted Muddlers and start catching char in rapid succession. They're all beautiful fish and all more or less the same size and shape—plump bordering on corpulent. One of them coughs up a heap of scuds, which explains their fatness and portends a particularly succulent lunch: Few fish are as sweet as those finished on crustaceans. We fish for a few hours and, after dozens of fish, retire to a shady island to build our lunch fire.

There's a deep comfort in the sizzle of four whole char baking over a wood fire, especially if those chars' bellies have been plumped with black morels and spruce tips. The eating is a revelation in the literal sense of the word: All respective sets of bones are picked clean, first with jack-pine chopsticks, then greedy fingers. Afterward I go down to the water with the carcasses and look out over the lake. The sun is soft and warm and there's a feeling that, this time, the warmth is here to stay. The blackflies agree. They aren't quite eating me alive yet, but they are getting some mighty good bites in.

I toss the brook trout spines into the water and immediately they're sieged by minnows, a swarm so sudden and thick you'd think they had some piranha DNA. It strikes me how quickly these bits of brook trout will find their way back into brook trout—quite possibly this evening when the big fish come shallow to hunt these little scavengers. The Canadian Shield in the springtime is a hungry country, where bits and pieces of one thing find their way all too quickly into the next. This is perhaps the greatest charm and utility of backcountry fishing—the way it clarifies connections between the world's creatures, all losing and gaining themselves at turns. Sometimes the food, sometimes the fed. And sometimes—I swat at a blackfly and dab at a dribble of blood—both at once.

IV. The End

Finally we come to the end. On our last morning we get up extra early and load all the gear onto the pontoon that will ferry us to the train depot. I'm down one camo Croc and a pint of blood, though I've made up for my loss with the kind of extra poundage that comes from eating lodge dessert every night for a week straight. The train is late, but the blackflies are not; this makes for a particularly active form of waiting. Each man attempts a different defense against the bloodthirsty marauders. Dan dons all his layers and covers his face, losing triple in sweat what he otherwise would in blood. Tom takes out his camera and attempts to capture visually pleasing constellations of the critters—the sublimation defense. Brian opts for a more aggressive tactic, loading his vape to the hilt and doing his best dragon imitation.

At long last the train shows up. I lean my head against the window and try to count moose in the swamps blurring by, far more soporific than sheep. And just as on loud, windy nights when you're camped in the middle of nowhere, phantom sounds start to emerge from the white noise of the tracks: the scream of a good fish putting a hurt on the drag, the clunk of the cedar boat hitting dock, the wet thunder of a big pike as it breaches. And as I slip into sleep there's a new sound too—not quite a murmur and not quite a shush—the sound of all the unfished shield water calling out to me, calling after me, as the train hauls east toward home.

CHAPTER 8

❧

The San River: A Love Story

"Son."

The confectioner leaned out of his brightly colored booth, closer, then closer again. In his outstretched hand, a chocolate-covered banana trembled just inches from my face.

"Son?"

"David," my mother growled, shaking my 11-year-old shoulder to return me from whatever unavailable frequency I was on to the Taste of Chicago, Dessert Island, 1991.

"He's in love," the vendor winked at me as I blankly accepted the treat.

I blinked. I was in fact not in love but rather thinking through a new and elaborate catfish rig involving a pair of wine corks, a maze of hooks, and a proprietary scent-delivery system (pantyhose, chicken liver). But I didn't correct him, just shrugged my shoulders and slinked away mutely, the same way I would years later when the restaurant manager asked who in the world forgets a twelve top, or when my first serious girlfriend questioned how it's possible to get lost for an hour in the IKEA parking lot, or when my department chair wanted to know what I was scribbling at so intently that I didn't realize the unit meeting had ended. In such circumstances I knew it was better to keep quiet and not reveal the truth, that I was debating whether to fish the strip mine or creek mouth, or pondering the best winging material for a winter steelhead fly, or itemizing possessions I could sell to afford a month's fishing in New Zealand. And while I mostly accepted such departures from reality as the natural and inescapable functioning of my brain, in certain moments of direr crisis I would find myself wondering, with a combination of anxiety and shame, how it was that I'd wound up with this janky brain whose default setting was fish. Where had this cognitive defect come from? Who or what was to blame?

It was on a mission to answer this question that I found myself at the age of 32 on a bridge over Poland's San River, standing beside an idling rental car and watching the riseforms of hundreds of grayling as they darned themselves to the film. I was here to fish in the footsteps of my paternal ancestors who had lived along the San and its tributaries for centuries before emigrating to the U.S. during and after the Second World War. Here I'd seek an answer to this lifelong obsession with water. Here I'd look for the source of my infatuation with fish. In the best-case scenario I saw myself discovering a clear piscatorial forefather, some riparian Rain Man or secret Slavic Walton, but I would've been happy with even a little tidbit, the smallest clue as to why, generations later on the other side of the world, the family genes had given rise to such a fish-obsessed fool.

I'd begin my detective work on the river, but first I had to get to it—which was not as easy as it would seem. The manager at the lodge I was staying at explained that I would need to buy a ticket for every day I wanted to fish, and that they were only sold by the conservation officers who worked the river. He then gave me two phone numbers. I sighed but was not surprised. If there's one thing I've learned in my years on the water, it's that the best fishing in any region is guarded in its own unique way. In the State of Wisconsin the cold-water fisheries have the twofold problem of being very small and very accessible by car, so there prevails a mix of silence and perplexity when someone inquires about the fishing. "Trout? In this state?" That is, of course, unless you meet someone rod-in-hand at your spot, or they find you in theirs, at which point there flares up an almost embarrassing level of intimacy, and you leave the water with a few new flies and a few new spots, having contributed the same.

Anglers in Michigan covet their best water via the art of misdirection, which might find them talking very loudly but incorrectly about where they'd caught a given fish, a subterfuge that funnels anglers to certain very well-atomized rivers. Great are the lengths they will go. I remember once being on a great mousing river as my friend tried to keep his shoulder in its socket while a twenty-nine-inch brown trout rolled on the other end of his Boga. "Don't get that background in the photo," he told me as he waved at an area directly behind him. "But stand over there and get that willow. It looks like a spot on the Au Sable."

In Europe, where there is no secret water, exorbitantly priced day tickets are the norm for keeping out the hoards. Poland follows this protocol on all its quality trout water, but the San fishery managers kick it up a notch by limiting the number of day-ticket vendors to two and putting them in motion: upriver or down, fishing or napping, running errands or at dinner, their cell phones on or off. I spent my entire first morning tracking down one of these gatekeepers, ultimately finding him at lunch with his in-laws in the center of a medieval town some ten kilometers from the river. For fifteen minutes I stood in the doorway vaping butter and onions while he filled out a week's worth of tickets. It was tough to tell beneath his small mammal of a mustache, but when he handed over my permits I thought I detected a smile of approval at my effort.

It was finally time to hit the river of my ancestors, a rite I performed with much gravitas and fanfare, including but not limited to doing a shot of vodka with the river and penning a few rather purple verses, the first poetry I'd written since college. But if I harbored any illusions that this ancestral home water would accept me with open eddies—and I most certainly did—I was disabused of that fact after just one hour of fishing. Despite being surrounded by dozens if not hundreds of rising fish, I was able to capture just a few smaller browns, which were not only the wrong size, but the wrong species. Today I was after grayling, European grayling to be exact, not the over eager *Thymallus arcticus* found throughout North America but the rarefied and aristocratic *Thymallus thymallus*. I had never caught a grayling of any type, and given the suspected ubiquity of grayling in the lives and diets of my forebears, I wondered if catching one would trip some pivotal mechanism in my DNA and express some latent trait that hadn't yet surfaced.

I fished on, and on. By late afternoon I found myself at a sharp bend in the river beyond which lay several dozen brightly colored wooden structures no larger than the average American toolshed but nonetheless possessing the accouterments of proper living quarters—windows and porches with potted plants and rocking chairs. Was it some sort of sacred elving ground? A witness-protection program for Polish grandmothers? I would never know, since suddenly I came face-to-face with my first truly large grayling, the kind of fish that rearranged the atoms in my body and toward which I felt an existential compulsion to conquer. In me the prodigal genes had finally come home, and it was time for this fish to know it.

On my first drift the great fish came within an inch of my bug, then tucked away behind the billowing cloak of its dorsal fin, like a vampire shirking sunlight behind its cape. It was all downhill from there. Over the next hour I cycled through every reasonable fly in my box, then clipped and trimmed failed offerings into more appetizing shapes. I went down to 7X, then 8X. I considered using a single strand of human hair as tippet. To solve the problem of micro-drag, I sunk a size 22 R2 dropper. Already closer than I should have been, I stepped a few more feet toward the fish.

Tom McGuane wryly observed that fishing takes a lot of time and that that was indeed the point, but what fishing does with all the time it takes is something less scrutinized and perhaps not very well understood. It's been my experience that brook trout fishing can in fact add time to a day, which means that your average *Salvelinus* angler has lived well beyond his years, and certain small-stream practitioners in the Upper Peninsula of Michigan may be as old as Noah. Muskie fishing tenderizes time, which is the only way I can explain how quickly and easily it goes down once a great *masquinongy* strikes (I often remember only the eat and the release). My pursuit of this

San River grayling, on the other hand, inserted time into some sort of compacting machine, a metaphysical variant of those megaton devices that smash whole automobiles into briefcase-size blocks of steel. Big hour-long chunks of time I experienced as mere Chiclets, and the more intently I worked the fish, the more time seemed to compress. When evening fell and my quarry took to eating nymphs subsurface, I was still there beside it, my back bent like the business end of a hockey stick, watching its smoky emerald form flash forward as the river went dark.

The following morning I was wadering up near an older gentleman and telling him, in my pidgin Polish, all about the previous day's shortcomings. Whether he took pity on my clunky tongue or fishing failure or both is hard to say, but when I showed him my fly box—a very typical Michigander's fly box, I might add, with the fibers of many large land mammals well represented in the materials list—he just shook his head. Opening his own box, he very slowly, very deliberately picked out a half-dozen dry flies and uncupped them into my palm. I squinted. They were those maddening Eastern European parachute patterns that looked like they had been made by gnomes: tiny but perfectly tapered quill bodies and single turns of the sparsest rooster hackle you'd ever seen, all on a hook so thin it looked like an overly curved eyelash. They appeared too frail to stop light. I wondered, as I stared at them in my hand, if on a windy day they would even land.

But the flies worked, and I'm pleased to credit that gentleman— Janek or Slawek or possibly Tadek—with an assist for my first San River grayling, a beautiful fish in the respectable fourteen-inch range. Staring at it in the net I saw that what I had originally taken for a single hue was actually a vector for many different colors, dark greens and blacks and reds and purples, as if the fish had been dipped in motor oil and dredged in chippings from the inside of an oyster shell.

It was two days of good fishing later before my basic Maslowian need for a bent rod was fulfilled and I was free to take care of other business, like meeting some of my fellow anglers, who had the habit of gathering in some of the riverside huts to sit out a drizzle and drink a beer or tea. They were from all over Europe, like a UN conference dressed in Gore-Tex. I met a number of Poles, including a small cadre of big trout hunters from Warsaw, one of whom had tattooed on his back an elaborate mural of a fiercely kyped brown trout going airborne after a mayfly dun escaping via his neck. They told me they knew a river where the biggest fish in the country swam, apprehensible only by throwing huge terrestrial patterns in broad daylight, and that they would consider taking me there at some point. I left them my card.

Then there was the British bachelor party that had come to the country in unapologetic pursuit of fishing and sex. Though three days into their trip, the partyers had not yet come to the realization that, here among the rolling hills and goat herds, these two goals were not to be achieved in the same locality.

I spent several consecutive afternoons fishing with a very intelligent and affable Ukrainian named Yuri, an optometrist from L'viv who when I asked how long he would be fishing the San replied, "Until the war with Russia is over."* He explained that things were going so poorly in the conflict that they were even looking to draft middle-age eye doctors who had never operated anything more dangerous than an air puffer machine. During one of our conversations, we were discussing the recent downing of a Malaysian passenger jet when he hooked into a twenty-six-inch rainbow trout. On releasing the fish, he said something I didn't know whether to attribute to fishing or to war: "Many things seem impossible, until they aren't."

And finally there was the river itself, which I did shots with on at least two other occasions and whose habits and patterns I was beginning to divine, from its cycle of daily hatches to its performance

---

* The events in this essay take place in 2014, at the very beginning of the Russian-Ukrainian conflict.

of evening fog, a ghostly phenomenon distantly related to the aurora borealis. One day it would come oozing down the riparian corridor like a river of foaming yeast; another day it would manifest in crisp triangular shapes, like pyramids of smoke. One evening during a gloomy rain the sun popped out and pressed the fog into a low, flat band of the sort you find around planets, hazy at the edges and bright as enamel in the middle. Whatever the shape, when the fog overtook you it blurred the world dreamily, and it became easy to imagine what this river was like long ago, perhaps in the time of the ancient Celts who first settled the river and gave it the name San, meaning "fast-flowing water," or in the Middle Ages when the tribal peoples of Hungary, Poland, and Kievan Rus fought for dominion over the fertile river valleys, or in the time my late grandmother lived here—exactly a century ago at the time of this writing—standing in the water washing clothes and singing the songs she'd recite decades later in a place she'd probably never heard of until she escaped to it after the Second World War: Indiana.

One such foggy evening I was on a new and remote stretch of river when my reverie was interrupted by a riseform of a type and magnitude I hadn't yet seen on this trip, one of those slow, deliberate porpoisings that make one think of monsters who live in lochs—one hump for its shoulders and one for its tail. I saw another good fish upstream and two farther down. Not able to see what the fish were feeding on, I tied on a size 6 stimulator with an unweighted Brown Drake nymph dropper. When I looked up from my knot work I saw that the entire river was seething with large trout. The first fish I cast to, which might have been the biggest rising fish I'd ever seen, ate so voraciously I couldn't tell if it took the dry or dropper or both. My rod doubled over, the fish pulled for a logjam, I pulled back, it was gone—all in the span of a second or two. My busted leader hung there trailing in the breeze like spittle.

One of the peculiarities the hook and bullet sports have over more formalized pursuits like tennis or shuffleboard is the suddenness with which glory or grief becomes available. One moment absolutely nothing is happening, the next you're entwined with the quarry of a lifetime, and there's no way to predict or prepare for the surprise. This process—akin to getting yanked off the couch and put up to bat with a full count and runners on in the bottom of the ninth—asks a lot of the nervous system. Hit a grand slam and there's nothing like it. Whiff spectacularly and there is your mortality affirmed. *You only get so many shots of fish like that in a lifetime*, a voice inside me said as I stood there processing what had just happened. *And this is one you're not getting back.*

Luckily, the sickness is also the cure, so I retied my leader thicker and stronger and scoured my fly box for a redemption bug. The porpoises of fish eating emergers had been replaced by the sharp surface slurps of fish taking duns, and I could finally see that the bug in question was a very large pale mayfly, about a size 8. My heart both quickened and smiled as I tied on a *Hexagenia* pattern. If there was one thing this Midwesterner knew how to do, it was throw dry flies the size of hummingbirds at big trout in the dark.

In the thickening dusk I sounded out the best riser in my vicinity, timed its eats, and made a good cast. Shutting out all other sounds, I listened only to the slot of river directly in front of me. Nothing, nothing, then *boom*, a percussion that subwoofed right through my chest. The fish took off downstream as if it had jumped a train to Krakow. Having already lost one great fish, I made the executive decision— somewhat questionable in daylight, downright dubious at dusk—of giving chase through water I did not know. I hurdled invisible sweepers, I tiptoed over rolling cobble, I ballerina'd over pockets of water so deep my boot tips barely ticked bottom. But my rod never came unbent, and five minutes later I was still alive and with a trout in hand, a gorgeous hen brown trout, fat as a barrel, with all the oversize, well-defined markings of a leopard.

It was only after resuscitating the fish that I realized how deep a pickle I was in. The sky was dark, the river was swift and wide, and the only safe crossing I knew of was upstream. Far upstream. What had taken five minutes to accomplish while tethered to a wild animal took twenty-five minutes of mincing boot tips to undo. The long slog served as a powerful reminder of my tendency to get lost in fishing at the expense of other things, and I realized I was halfway through my trip and hadn't yet started looking for any family members or evidence thereof. If I was going to try and find an angling antecedent in the gnarled branches of the family tree, it was time to get down to it.

For the next two days I slept in, healed wounds, ate too much steak tartar (the only way I can get enough), and walked about the town of Sanok gathering information about the possible whereabouts of relatives. My findings suggested I should focus on the Ukrainian branch, the Chnatushkos, who I knew only through my paternal grandmother, a strong and proud woman who used to regale me as a young boy with bedtime stories of wolves at the door and who bragged of once defeating the devil in a fistfight. If any branch of the family tree held a fishing freak, it would likely be these demon brawlers from the eastern side of the San.

Finding them, however, would not be easy. After the Second World War, the newly installed Soviet government relocated all ethnic minorities to different parts of Poland and Ukraine in order to make the populations more tractable. If any Chnatushkos had returned to the San River valleys, my best bet for finding them would be to attend a Ukrainian-language service at one of the Orthodox churches, or *cerkiews*, that dotted the hillsides.

And so Sunday morning I was out driving early enough to see the sunlight planking over the mountains, beams of light so sturdy you felt you could walk on them. There was something different in the air here on the other side of the San, and I found myself thinking back to what an older Pole had told me earlier in the month: "On the other side of the San, Asia begins." Prior to the first two world wars, this region had been a melting pot where many different groups—Poles, Jews, Ukrainians, Roma, and Russians—lived together in relative peace. Barszcz, clear and rubescent, lived next door to borscht, milky and bean-pegged. Village edicts were written in the Roman alphabet, Cyrillic, and Hebrew. On Sunday mornings ethnic Poles would pass in and out of brick Roman Catholic churches in the town squares, while farther out in the forest, ethnic Ukrainians shuffled into thousand-year-old wooden *cerkiews* with onion-shaped domes.

After an hour of slow driving down a dirt-packed river road, I finally came across my grandmother's old village, a sleepy mountain hamlet of old stone homes, wandering geese, plum orchards, and poppy fields. I approached a group of men taking their morning vodka on the hood of an orange Fiat and asked about the nearest *cerkiew*. They made me drink a shot with them, after which I followed a guy on a Soviet-era motor scooter and a ratty Uncle Sam T-shirt to the bottom of a heavily wooded hill with no steps, only a dirt path with a makeshift rail of old branches nailed to tree trunks. The *cerkiew* sat on the top of the hill with a 360-degree view of the mountains. I was late, and the sound of singing was already wafting out the open door into the morning air. As I entered, I was overwhelmed by the smell of myrrh and the glitter of gold. Though I was only the fifteenth or so person in this small wooden space, no one interrupted their singing or turned to look at me when I entered. Having been raised Catholic, I was accustomed to the Sunday acoustics of brick and stone in massive spaces. But the tenor of the human voice sounded much different in this confined space, reverberating off the bones of an ancient forest. It was warm—honeyed even—like singing inside of a violin.

After the service was over, I loitered in the courtyard until an older gentleman handed me a cigarette and observed that I was not from around here. When I told him I was looking for my grandmother's people he nodded and closed his eyes: "Yes, I knew the Chnatushkos." He introduced me to several other churchgoers and invited us all to his small home, where we spent hours eating hot chicken soup and fresh pork cutlets and listening to stories of the First World War and Second World War and smaller wars without names, of those who survived and those who didn't, of those who had returned and those who were never heard from again. The Chnatushkos, all could affirm, had not come back. There was my grandmother who had escaped to the United States. Her brother who'd been relocated west to the newly acquired land from Germany. A few cousins who'd been sent east to Ternopil in what is now Ukraine. They couldn't say whether there were any sportsmen in the family, and due to all the farmwork, they did not suspect anyone had had the opportunity to develop much facility with a fishing rod. They did remember that the local children liked to tickle fish out from shady cutbanks on sunny days, and that the Chnatushkos would have been among them.

When all the stories had gone to embers, with the teapot empty and the bread stale, I pushed away from the table, shook hands, and left. But I only drove a short way, stopping near the base of a low mountain where I'd been told my grandmother's house had once sat. Whatever it had been, it was now all overgrown field and dense forest. There was no road, no path, no way forward or deeper. I thought back to the time I had spent a whole day trying to find the source of one of my favorite Wisconsin brook trout streams. Just when the river had tapered to a narrow trickle and I thought I was closing in on the source, I rounded a bend and saw it spring open into a hundred watery fluoresces. Rather than finding one source, I'd found infinite beginnings. Rather than tapering to a final answer, there was just a burst of new questions.

For my very last two days on the San I hired a guide. I felt good about my DIY bushwacking, and the browns and grayling I'd managed to catch on my own had given me a sense of accomplishment. I could now take orders from someone else without getting rankled; if my guide told me to nymph all day on a short line, I would nymph all day on a short line. There was no way to know if I would ever be back, and I wanted to make sure I had experienced the full depth of the fishery. I didn't want to find myself wondering, "What if?"

My guide arrived from Krakow the next day. His name was Mirek, and he was a tall, thin, serious individual with a diverse collection of beer he kept in an electric cooler still quite a bit of R&D away from competing with actual ice. But the temperature of the beer was made up for by its constant availability. In Poland, anyone but the driver is allowed to be in whatever state of intoxication the situation requires. Now that I was no longer driving, the situation required constant festivity.

We quickly passed the general area I'd been fishing that week—"boring water that everyone knows," Mirek said. Soon we were driving down a warren of dirt roads that ran through sheep pastures and beet farms, occasionally crossing small tributaries, all the while rising and falling on low hills like the stylus on a warped record. The half-keyless BlackBerry the lodge manager had loaned me buzzed every few minutes to welcome us to another country: Poland, then Slovakia, then Ukraine, then Poland again. We finally stopped in front of a farm with overgrown sunflowers and tumbled over beehives, where Mirek showed me how to kick a wild boar in case we were accosted in the forest. In an emerald tributary on our way to the river, we startled a pair of mushroom hunters cleaning a huge haul of fat boletes. I recognized the wild glint in their eyes—it was the look of two hunters whose catch had vastly exceeded their expectations.

When we finally arrived at the river, wide as a football field and flat as a glass tabletop, my first thought was confusion: How didn't I notice it was raining? Then I realized it wasn't rain but the riseforms of hundreds of trout and grayling. The water was so calm and clear, so shallow and slow that you could see not only their sips but the fish beneath them, quavering puddles of liquid silver and copper that would float up toward tiny mayflies that would never lift off to the safety of the air.

"You said you wanted a challenge," Mirek said.

My initial entry into the river pushed a wake that put all the fish down within twenty yards. "Slowly," Mirek cautioned. I waited a few minutes and started again, this time using the slowest movements, the same way I used to eat the pierogi my Ukrainian grandmother would make for me when I was a child. She'd carefully baste each dumpling with melted butter, not stopping until the liquid rose up to the edges of my plate and the golden surface bulged. The only way to eat them without making a mess was to cut them with the greatest, tenderest care.

"David," Mirek warned suddenly. "Do not move. Do not even tilt your head. There is a huge grayling directly behind you."

I moved so slowly it took four breaths to turn my head sideways. The grayling was so close I could see its eyes when it rose.

Too close to risk the motions of a cast, I gathered my leader and a few feet of fly line in my free hand and started feeding it out a little at a time, dropping the line at my knees. One clump. Two clumps. Three. I couldn't focus on both my hands and drift at once, so I relied on Mirek to tell me what was going on.

"Good, good, good . . . now!"

I set the hook by stabbing the line in my hand firmly upriver, as if daggering a king. The grayling was there, heavy and angry. I like to think I carried myself with great poise through this battle, but the fact is I fell twice chasing the fish—I think. All I really remember is Mirek's shouting—"Huge grayling! Huge grayling!"—and that his rolled *r*'s gave the fish an extra syllable. Finally it was in the net. In the sunlight the fish was all opalescence, its muscular body glittering black-green here, blue-pink there. Only its rippling dorsal fin kept a constant color, the burnt red of old blood. We admired it, congratulated each other, snapped a picture, and watched it slink away. And as it faded into the slow waters of the San, Mirek put his hand on my shoulder and opened his mouth to say something.

I'll never know what it was.

That's because in the middle of that perfect moment, with both of us feeling on top of the top of the world, something wholly unnecessary and stupidly spectacular happened.

A huchen breached.

Whether it was chasing a brown trout for dinner or simply wanted to take a short flight I couldn't say, but when those three feet of freshwater salmon left the river they made an unripping sound, and when they landed, the boom waked all the way to our boots.

Suddenly the grayling was history, and the look of satisfaction on Mirek's face was replaced with the kind of deadly seriousness you might expect before embarking on a dangerous mission you are not likely to survive. "I go for huchen rod," he blurted and disappeared into the brush, leaving me with two warm bottles of beer and a few hundred rising fish. All was so quiet you could hear the bee working the flower beside you, or the blip of a grayling eating at fifty feet, or the fizz of beer in a freshly opened bottle.

It was by all counts and measures as perfect a moment as I've ever experienced.

I didn't fish as I waited for Mirek's return. If anything, I wanted this moment between casts to widen, for the distance to the car to keep increasing, for my bottle of beer to never quite empty. And as I wallowed in the moment, it occurred to me that maybe I had been going about this family detective business all wrong. Whether or not they had ever cast a line, I knew my ancestors had spent countless hours staring out over the San while tending animals, while walking to church, while waiting for armies to pass. And maybe in the same way a river could cut a bank and shape a channel, a river flowing past your eyes and ears and nose day in and day out could carve its way into your brain, could wire not only you but those that came after you with a soft spot for water. With an eye for the play of light in a riffle. With a belief in the eternal promise of a riverbend.

With a kind of love, perhaps.

CHAPTER 9

The Middle Fork of Stupid Good

ALL ANGLERS NEED THE ODD FREAKISHLY GOOD DAY. SUCH DAYS clear the system of junk, an angioplasty for the fishing soul. They needn't be frequent to be useful. The momentum generated by a single day of exceptional fishing can carry over months and even years, buoying you aloft when you need to wake before dawn to fish flies as small as a birthmark, or goading you along to swap a perfectly good campfire for a long wade under a new moon, alone but for the coal-black mouse tethered to your 0X. Yes, the occasional day of ridiculous fishing sustains the optimism all anglers need to remain inoculated against golf, competitive birdwatching, things of that nature. But what if one day you recognized yourself a broken angler, one with an urgent medical need for not just one but a fistful of stupid good days?

This was my recent predicament. Owing to one of the more inclement springs on record, my home-state fishing had been not so much a mixed bag as an empty sack. The spring rains came early, stayed late, and in their ferocity seemed intent on returning the Michigan mainland to the inland sea from which it came. All our great watersheds went high and muddy; not a tributary was spared. Riffles disappeared. Boulders dislocated. Old sweepers migrated downstream, and new ones fell from the bank. The trout, oblivious to the anguish of the thousands of anglers who lived to drift bugs above them, hunkered away under timber and filter-fed on earthworms.

Despite these abominable conditions, I fished as hard as I ever had, driving through two tire rotations and chasing minor windows of opportunity whenever they were to be found. The results were abysmal, however, and after three decades of fishing I was starting to lose the one thing more essential to angling than the angle: hope. So in early July, after weeks of waiting on a hex hatch that never materialized, I got on a plane bound for Alaska. To rehabilitate my angling heart. To repair my fishing soul. To get back in touch with what the old reptilian part of my brain knew, deep down, fishing was supposed to be.

Project Salvation, as I had taken to calling it, would take place in Alaska's Bristol Bay region, the most diverse horn of piscine plenty I have yet encountered in my medium-length life, and thus the best bet for a bedraggled angler looking to turn their fortunes around. Arriving at my lodge on a Saturday evening, our host gave us a rundown of the week: a different fly out every day; good fishing for resident rainbows, grayling, dollies; still waiting on a good push of kings to get that program going. My soul uncurdled a little. Finally, a week of fishing that might not only take me out of the red, but put me deep in the black.

Our first day would be spent at what the guides referred to as "the narrows," a short stretch of shallow, swift water between two large lakes. Often the first day of a lodge program is a bit of a set piece, an easy gimme, something to slake the thirst of guests and prime them for the more complex opportunities to come. Over the roar of the de Havilland my guide explained to me that the narrows this week were chock full of salmon fry, and all-day long wave upon wave of hungry dollies, grayling, and lake trout would press in from the lakes above and below, compressing the fry until they formed dense balls of flesh the predators would slash into with open mouths. After a half-hour flight the plane set down on a creamy blue lake with a wide cobble beach. From here it was a short walk to our fishing.

This was not my first time in Alaska, but I was still awestruck by the sheer quantity of fish before me. If all the trout were suddenly removed from my home waters—heck, throw in all the suckers too—river levels would not drop one iota. But take all the fish out of the narrows and I expect its volume would drop by half. Fish were everywhere. Wade out into position and in the time it took you to tie on a fly, a dozen fat fish would file into the seam forming behind your legs. Head to the bank for a beer, or push out into deeper water to chase a distant fry bust, and fish would cram into the spot you just left, like feckless commuters on a crowded bus.

Catching these skinny water fry-busters required a different kind of hatch-matching—"dry fry fishing," the guides called it. Basically, you wait for one of the hundreds of char or grayling to bust up on a fry ball in your vicinity, then cover it up immediately with a bushy dry fly and an inch-long Gummy Fry dropper. A dead-drift worked best—it was really the only way to distinguish your offering from the thousands of fleeing naturals—and you usually saw the take in the form of a violent roil beneath the dry. Grayling were particularly prone to eating this way. Other times you'd observe a big char stabbing forward beneath your dry fly like a thick blue sword, twisting and glinting in the sunlight as it goes in for the kill. Every few fish, I'd pause to rub the forearm of my rod hand, which was still in spring-training mode. I wondered how well it would hold up as the week wore on and whether this was why the lodge kept a massage therapist on staff.

On the flight back to the lodge, the question of where we would fish the next day was an open debate. It was solved when one of our party, a Montanan whose wife had been the hot hand that day, pressed his finger against the window of the Beaver as we flew over a perfect little creek. "What's that?" he asked. "Can we fish there?" The plane canted and dropped in low to give us all a better look at the water. At that height the boulders looked like pinheads and the sockeye, if your prescription was up to date, looked like mosquito larvae. "That's Contact Creek," the pilot said. "And the answer, of course, is of course."

Such is the beauty of having a thousand different places to fish that no one had yet fished Contact that year, which only added to the intrigue and conjecture over the next day's morning coffee. After ballasting with salmon hash and poached eggs with hollandaise sauce (this writer does not acknowledge oatmeal's right to exist in Alaska, though the lodge humors those who do), we loaded the Beaver with 6-weights and were off. After an hour's flight and a landing in a tundra puddle that, I learned, was big enough to land on but not take off from (with a full load of passengers, at least), I asked my guide how far off the river was. He paused thoughtfully. "As long as there are no bear issues, we'll be on the water in fifteen minutes."

On the ground, the river we'd seen from above was invisible. There was only a chest-high sea of alders stretching to the mountains on the horizon. But look down at the trail beneath your feet and you saw bear sign. A lot of bear sign. The Russian playwright Anton Chekhov once said a gun that appears in the first act of a play must go off in the fifth. I'd put forth an Alaskafied version, that if your path to the river is so full of bear scat it looks like someone had been off-roading in a dump truck full of charcoal, you will be high-holed by multiple horribili before your first water break. Our first bear, a midsize lumbering male with a long neck and a sad face, made us all pause and look for escape routes until we saw that he was singularly interested in sockeye. After that our only response when bears came close was to stop fishing, since the odds of hooking a fish on any given cast were roughly 50/50, and no griz needed the temptation of easy food on a string.

Our party fished dries until lunch and had good-enough fishing, but it wasn't until I crept up a narrow side channel and started fishing subsurface that it would become the kind of day that realigns the neurons in your brain and endows you with the sort of grin that the English language, in one of its stranger moves, associates with coprophagia. There I stood, staring at a blue sluice of water between two boulders. It was deep enough that you couldn't see bottom, and sufficiently broken that you couldn't spot a big rainbow even if you knew exactly where it was holding. It was a familiar type of water, a variation on a theme I knew from fishing the plunge pools of southwest Wisconsin's spring creeks—dark, fast slots into which you'd send a tungsten scud like a message in a bottle and see who wrote back. I didn't come to Alaska to fish nymphs, however, so I tied on a simple marabou sculpin with a tungsten head, worked some spit into the marabou so the first cast counted, and dropped it upstream of my position. Almost tight-lining it, I followed the path of the jig with my rod tip, paying close attention to the water as my fly bobbed in and out of view, in and out of view, in and out of view—and then it was gone.

A rainbow trout's take on its home turf is a beautiful thing. Deep in the turquoise churn, the water flinches and your fly disappears, reborn a millisecond later as an arcing mykiss, its pie-tin back and crimson stripe flashing in stark relief against the pale tundra. I was in no way ready for that first fish, which broke its tether fifty yards downstream. But I was ready for the next one, and the next. For the remainder of the afternoon I hunted out deep, blue fast water, and from each pulled a fish that dared me to break my ankles giving chase over broken cobble. Now I have always been an excitable boy with a rod in my hands. High on the list of things I have never learned to do is keep my composure in the face of exceptional fishing. I hoot, I holler, I cry out for a helmet and a chaperone. Back home, my fishing mates tell me to keep it down. But here in the land of the griz, my carrying on whenever fast to a fish had the bonus function of clearing any and all *Ursus* from the area. Thus did I sally forth all day long, cheered on by my comrades as I plowed my way downstream, a human bear banger with a chronically bent rod.

By the midpoint of the trip I was starting to even my ledger for the year, not only in terms of fish, but novelty of experience. Every day presented a different body of water, a different style of fishing, a different series of snapshots through the window of the Beaver: bonsai gardens of black spruce; meteor craters full of sapphire-blue water; bear trails like someone had dragged a garden rake across a pool table; beluga whales like grains of rice. The days did not blend together. There was the day on Kulik when we swang up rainbows all the livelong, punctuated by screaming drags and leopard-spotted cheeks. A day on Margaret when I caught dollies between positively Posturepedic naps on the tundra moss. The day we spent lining sockeye that we'd line our bellies with for the rest of the trip.

I knew I had turned a corner one day when instead of joining my compatriots for any afternoon of easy fishing—clobbering char rabid for eggs behind redded sockeyes—I snuck away to spend the afternoon casting at spooky grayling in tricky presentation windows. I'd cast between shady trees for two-foot drifts that would have them tipping back into sunlight as they followed the drift, only to refuse and disappear behind their rippling capes. With everyone else wearing out the disc drags on their reels, I went down to 5X mono. Then 6X fluoro. In my Moleskine I wrote purple passages of how noble it was to not catch fish.

It was very un-Alaska of me.

My guide left me to my technical devices for most of the day. But with an hour to go, he'd had enough.

"No more grayling," he said, firmly taking my rod from my hands before biting off my caddis and replacing it with a fluorescent foam mouse and egg dropper. "This is the craziest egg bite I've ever seen. You'll regret not hitting it. Fish your way back to the plane, and try to keep us in sight."

Now, I have done many Brook Trout Death Marches in my life—agonizing tramps through thick, buggy swamp that leave you looking like you'd been attacked by measles and cougars at the same time—but it wasn't until that last hour of mousing and egging dollies that I discovered it's equal and opposite reaction: the Downstream Dolly Relay. For over an hour I ran eggs through pods of char up to ten pounds that fought each other for my fly and then towed me downstream to the next pool, where they more or less handed me off to the next fish like a human baton. When I arrived at the plane an hour later, I was out of breath, punch-drunk, and in desperate need of a helmet. I accepted a beer instead.

❦

That night at the lodge, rumor had it that the first good push of kings had moved in, and we were one medium-length flight away from

THE MIDDLE FORK OF STUPID GOOD

intercepting them. Everyone spoke in low, excited tones over after-dinner cocktails. I was particularly excited, a good king being the one thing left on my itinerary.

By next morning, however, a front had settled in.

"Sorry," our host said. "No flying till we see sky."

I went outside with my coffee to see about the weather. It was mighty dark for ten o'clock in the morning, and foggy to boot. The mountains we'd stared at all week were guillotined at the shoulders by low clouds, and I could barely make out the floatplane at its mooring. I found the pilot sitting alone at the edge of the dock, mouthing an unlit stogie as he carved a cigar box out of driftwood.

"On days like this," he nodded sagely, "a pilot must have hobbies."

As the minutes became hours a few guests started eddying dangerously close to the wet bar, then a few more, and before you knew it ice was tinkling into glasses. You couldn't blame them. We'd enjoyed good fishing and fair weather for five days, and everyone was in high spirits. I myself wasn't keen to swap fish sorties for stories just yet, however, so rather than donning my Crocs and pouring a Seven & Seven, I slipped into waders and grabbed my 7-weight. Dress for the job you want and all that.

It worked. A bored-looking younger guide came up to me and asked if I wanted to fish the river mouth. "It's a few miles away on the other side of the lake," he said, pointing through his chest pockets. "There's a *really* good char crash. The smolt come out of the river into the lake in waves, and the char wait at the first deep drop. It's a half-hour ride by boat."

I mulled it over. Deciding how to spend one's last day in Alaska is not a simple decision, and this was complicated by the fact that I really, really wanted to swing up a king. During previous trips to Alaska I'd always missed out on connecting with one. They—or was it me?—were always too early or too late. Here the timing was finally right, but the weather was terribly wrong.

I looked down the dock at the pilot, who had portentously lit his cigar. There was no wind and the tobacco smoke plumed around him without budging.

"Char crash it is," I said.

We hopped in an eighteen-foot aluminum flat bottom with a plywood floor and jetted out across the big lake, the cold drizzle prickling my face as the miles ticked by. No matter what happened, I told myself as I cinched my jacket, it had been an excellent week. I'd twice come an inch or two shy of the world record catch-and-release grayling. I'd skated up big rainbows on riffle-hitched Muddlers. I'd seen bear and moose and ptarmigan and even a wolverine. There was really nothing left to prove.

In the foggy distance we saw birds, sparse at first but gradually thickening as we neared the river mouth. Gulls were massed in the thousands, calmly preening themselves and paying us no mind. There was so much white you could almost not see the water in places. It felt like being in a snow globe at rest.

I stood up and stripped out some fly line—very deliberately and very slowly. I'd seen this Hitchcock film before.

"Don't cast," my guide said. "Just be ready."

A minute passed. Then a few more. All was quiet. Night-before-Christmas still. Then, the great snow globe was shaken and the gulls erupted in a blizzard. Shrieking, they funneled toward a spot on the water roughly two hundred yards away, as if being sucked down into some cosmic porthole.

"Down!"

The jet screamed to life and suddenly I was holding tight to the gunwales and even tighter to my breakfast, trying to see where we were going as my glasses bounced around my face. When the engine stopped, I jumped up on the bow and cast into the froth of tails and fins and backs and snots, whacking a few screeching gulls in the process. I got bit three times before finally coming tight to a good char that would not be horsed by a 7-weight. By the time we had it in the net, the bay had again gone quiet, the birds still, the fish vanished. I could hear my own heartbeat.

Then it happened again, a hundred yards in the opposite direction.

"Down!" my guide yelled, and we were off to the races again.

We did this over and over again, landing solid char with each cataclysm of flesh. Sometimes the fury lasted long enough to catch two fish, sometimes three, but most often we'd land just one before the crash ebbed and another started to build. I'd experienced plenty of hand-over-fist fishing in my life, but this was entirely different. It was gold rush and ghost town in a minute-long window, thirty seconds of madness followed by such an empty calm you wondered if it hadn't been a hallucination. It was, I realized as the tally reached ten, twenty, thirty fish or more, *the* greatest fishing afternoon of my life. By the time the two-radio crackled to life, I had redeemed every skunk I'd experienced going back to 1998.

"Weather clearing," a voice at the other end said. "Does he want to fish kings?"

It was a good question. Stay or go, stay or go? As I was pondering what to do, a crash erupted just off the bow of the boat, and my mind flashed back to when I was 9 years old throwing bread to swarming carp at the local nature preserve. The preserve, tragically, did not allow fishing, and I had always gone home in tears, my hands trembling at the injustice. Here, decades later, I had a chance at redemption.

"We stay!" I declared, and set my fly once again into motion.

And so we fished out the rest of the afternoon, trading off crashes until we neared physical collapse, then went ashore to eat a few of the fallen. As the ruby fillets simmered in oil and garlic, I thought about what Michigan looked like five or six generations ago. Grayling by the thousands packed in train cars bound for Chicago and Detroit. Sturgeon stacked like timber on the banks of rivers. Passenger pigeons so thick they darkened the sky. Extinct. Endangered. Extinct. Sipping coffee after the meal, I was overcome by a feeling of gratitude that I'd been able, here in Alaska, to bear witness to the grandest mechanisms of life and death as they've played out for millennia, oblivious to human intervention and machination.

And just like that, my rehab assignment was over.

The timing could not have been more excellent. My Michigan friends reported that the rivers back home were finally stabilizing and fishing was decent to good. As such there was mousing to be done during the second half of summer. Tricos to chase as the mornings cooled. Streamers to swing between sits in the tree stand. After a mere week of Stupid Good fishing, I felt ready for any opportunity the rest of the sporting world might throw at me. A brook trout death march across the entire Upper Peninsula of Michigan didn't seem out of the question.

And it was all thanks to Alaska, that mostly roadless nirvana where your fishing and hunting dreams are more likely to come true than not. May we never take the Great Land for granted. May all of us forever take care of Alaska, so that Alaska may forever take care of us.

CHAPTER 10

❧

Kings of the Road

F. Scott Fitzgerald claimed a sure sign of genius was the ability to hold two mutually exclusive ideas in one's head at the same time, believing in them both with full conviction. If that's true, the closest I've come to sheer brilliance is a July evening five years ago, when my friend Jason and I pledged to hit the road on a fishing trip at 6:30am, then proceeded to sip porch beers until sunrise.

This was no poke down the road. The genius fishing trip in question required the dooziest doozy of a drive—fourteen hundred miles from Ann Arbor, Michigan, to Labrador City, Newfoundland, where we'd board an Otter for the Atikonak River and its hump-backed brook trout. At least, it was fourteen hundred miles for me, the Michigander. Jason had volunteered to drive and was only picking me up en route. His starting point? Atlanta, Georgia.

Yes, it was madness, a sojourn that should have had us involuntarily committed at the Canada–U.S. border. But it conferred something terrifically useful: an acute perspective on the differences between driving and flying when it comes to destination travel. And these differences are not simple matters of time or convenience. The two modes of moving do different things to your very soul.

The very act of modern air travel pounds a person's psyche down to a fraction of its original size. You wait in line, doff your shoes, gut your pockets, and fidget nervously with your boarding pass as five customs agents converge on your fly-tying vise like it's a detonation device. On the plane you must tap a stranger on the shoulder every time you need to take a leak, and for your suffering are gifted a small scoop of nuked pasta. After landing you pace anxiously around the baggage carousel wondering if this is the time—it happens to all anglers once—that your fishing gear will mistakenly end up in Topeka. This is all a fine program for the alien anthropologist tasked with recording the absurdities of being a human on a small and increasingly discombobulated planet. But, if the goal of travel is a freedom commensurate with the angling enterprise that awaits, you're plum out of luck, and no number of airport Bloody Marys can change that.

But a road trip—now that is a different story. Rather than suffer a hundred indignities, you rejoice in a thousand freedoms. You ferry across fjords beneath arrays of midnight stars, eat poutine in gas stations full of taxidermied timber wolves, drink coffee in the shadow of hydroelectric dams so tall they blot out the sun. You count moose between naps, you lose track of time in the long dust plumes of logging trucks on gravel roads wider than a blue whale is long. You stop to stretch and pee when you want, where you want, all the while watching the landscape get bigger and wilder—much like yourself.

In short, rather than shrivel us down, our travel across Ontario, Quebec, and Labrador on the open road built us up. And once we arrived at the river, there was a sense of having earned the experience: the Atikonak brook trout chomping caddis under alder branches, the Ouananiche chasing down skated Muddlers in the fast water, the big pike ripping up one foam mouse after another. And when, after a week of fat fish and northern lights, it was time to go home, still we kept getting larger, and not just because we were puffed and swollen from blackflies, or bloated from pork chops thick as a pre-internet phone book. It was because we didn't have to travel to an airport, which, after a long week of fishing, scrapes away all the wild goodness you've accrued just as surely as bottle of vinegar on a cast-iron pan. In the morning you're releasing a ten-pound lake trout that ate a streamer in two feet of crystal-clear water, and in the evening you are studying the menu at a Cinnabon. You go from the best of what the world has to offer, to the worst.

But not Jason and I. Not this time. After the fishing was over, we still had the long drive home to turn over memories, reflect on glory and failure, and plan the next trip. And unlike the airport angler who must conceal or neutralize their hard-won stench (I once flew home from Anchorage wearing three pairs of pants), we embraced ours to the point of connoisseurship.

"Old hamburger patty under a summer sun."

"With overnotes of dairy barnyard."

"I'm getting a little dried squid on the exhale, if that makes sense."

Make no doubt about it, we retained our kingly status during the entire ride home. We stretched our thirty-hour trip to forty. We sang and laughed until our tears mixed with the fluids weeping from our blackfly wounds. We stopped twice as often as our drive out, stood leprously in line for coffee after coffee after coffee. And then a day and some hours later, on the midnight outskirts of Toronto, we decided it was time for a proper sleep and found a spot at the back of a dimly lit gas station parking lot.

Jason called dibs on the back of the CRV and burrowed himself into a cocoon of rod tubes, damp waders, and fly boxes, rolling around like a dog in a gut pile until he found a configuration he liked. I popped out for a nightcap of Molson and potato chips before settling into my front-seat sleeping quarters. And as I listened to the semis roar by in the distance, I realized that we were not only physically halfway home; we were also at a metaphysical halfway point. I could still smell brook trout slime on my arms and pick black spruce needles out of my hair, could still hear the churn of the Atikonak over the boulders and see the northern lights curtained across the sky. But I could also check in on the latest Packers transactions on my phone and cram my belly full of all the finest fruits of civilization, by which I mean Canadian potato chips in all colors of the savory rainbow: Maple Bacon, Montreal Smoked Meat, Scalloped Potatoes, Cowboy BBQ Beans.

And that's when I realized what a proper fishing road trip really is: a gentle double taper of a journey with a transformation at either end. Heading out, the tame man becomes wild; heading back, the wild creature is tamed. But it's such a slow process that, for a while at least, the feral creature and the civilized human sit across from each other, staring eye to eye, in the same body. And that's how I drifted off to sleep that night, on the edge of Ontario's Fertile Crescent, straddling two worlds and seeing both more clearly than before, sipping my Molson with the window rolled down just a crack, listening to all the life flowing by.

CHAPTER 11

Vision Quest

I.

"Do you see it?"

This is the fifth time my guide has asked this same question, and I'm trying, as I stare out over the wind-riffled water, to come up with a fresh answer. I've already been through *no*, *uh-uh*, *nada*, *sorry*, and I'm running out of ideas. It's not like I can't seeing *anything*, mind you. In fact, my problem may well be the opposite, that after a summer of travel and fishing across Canada and Alaska, my retinal rods are in overdrive and I'm seeing *too much*: the green glow of land that is the Upper Peninsula in the distance, the plush flotilla of late summer clouds overhead, the saw-toothed water the color and clarity of a gin gimlet. The only thing missing is what I came here to see, to hunt, to catch—carp in arguably the greatest carp fishery on the planet.

"Twelve o'clock, thirty feet. Good fish. See it?"

I scrunch my eyes behind my polarized sunglasses, but it's no dice, so I opt for a jocular, light-hearted *nope*. Only there's nothing light-hearted about it. In no other form of fishing is the inability to see your quarry as much a death knell as in flats fly-fishing for carp, which requires perfectly delivered flies in the face of fish that can move in and out of casting range in three heartbeats—four if you're lucky. If someone calls attention to a trout stabbing its snout through the film to eat mayflies, I can't miss it, but with carp on the flats of Lake Michigan, where fish with brown or purple tinges might be cruising over a rocky bottom in five feet of water, I can follow the barrel of my guide's finger and still be left shaking my head.

"Two o'clock now, fifty feet. Leaving range. Needs to be a long cast."

"I see it!" I lie, in full fake-it-till-you-make-it mode, and kick my fly rod into motion. In case it isn't obvious, this is not the carp fishing I did as a kid back in Chicago. Back then, chasing carp meant pedaling the bike to the nearest retention pond, often near a construction site, and soaking kernels of sweet corn in water the color and viscosity of hot gravy. By contrast, I got to Beaver Island on the deck of a sun-drenched ferry after a dockside margarita, and instead of plumbing a mudhole flanked by bulldozers, I'm zipping around an island paradise that reminds me of Capri. Only instead of needling into grottos with a guy named Luigi, I'm trying to thread the carp needle with Austin Adduci, who takes carp so seriously he's got them tattooed on his forearms.

I shoot the fly line as far as I can at my make-believe fish, hoping against hope that I've stepped on the needle in the haystack, but the look on Austin's face tells me I'm still way, way off.

The carp on his forearms clench as he starts digging through his fly box. "Until you get your carp eyes, I'm putting you on bass detail."

II.

If you're new to fly fishing, you might not know that Beaver Island, Michigan, has become something of a North American mecca for fly anglers. Let me back up a bit. If you're new to fly fishing you might not know that chasing carp is one of the fastest-growing scenes in the sport; that it's *the* challenge the seen-it-all, caught-it-all guides across the region and beyond seek out on their days off; that having caught a carp on a fly is an indisputable badge of honor, indisputable because there is no such thing as a lucky fish. You might catch a trout by chance while swinging your nymph at the end of a poor drift, maybe even button a muskie by dragging a fly you can't cast behind the boat, but any carp taken on a fly is intentional, calculated, willed.

But carp are only part of the reason why some of the best, most ambitious anglers across the whole country make their way to North-ern Michigan every year. The other part is Beaver Island itself.

"We don't sell fudge and we keep our horses in the pasture, where they belong," is the curt answer I get from a local when I ask how Beaver Island is different from their rival isle, the much more conventionally touristy Mackinac Island. Driving around town with Austin after a few good hours of smallmouth fishing, it's suddenly clear that any comparison to Mackinac is moot. Beaver Island is much larger and much, much stranger, with moody island atmospherics that are part David Lynch and part Jimmy Buffet, with a little Hemingway thrown in for good measure.

"You can wear your seatbelt if you want," Austin tells me. "But people will think you're weird."

When I looked at other vehicles, all driving slowly, all waving to each other, pickups alternating with golfcarts alternating with what I suspect is the world's densest population of GEO Trackers, it becomes apparent that I am, indeed, the weird one. Here's what's not weird on Beaver Island: a guy with a trailer hitch on the *front* of his car, since he prefers to push, not pull, his boat around town; open coolers in the backseats of beatifically restored midcentury convertibles, as if Cuba had signed an advertising deal with Anheuser-Busch; a trapper who makes sure a goodly percentage of the island's coyotes turn into fashionable headwear and its beavers into beverage coozies; a neon-light martini glass the size of an NBA point guard in the window of a house built like a Spanish galleon; two trees on the edge of town festooned top to bottom in strange regalia, one full up entirely of shoes, the other of bras; and everywhere, from picnic tables in the beds of pickup trucks ("it's called boodling," Austin informs) to the army of one-speeds leaning against the sides of restaurants, the signs and symbols of people who've mastered the art of taking it slow.

And that's the other reason I'm here. When you've managed a life where fishing has turned into a kind of work, it means you may well need a reintroduction to the art of relaxation. I wonder if maybe, just maybe, my vision problems are due to my innards being wrapped up too tight.

"What's the Rx for someone who has problems slowing down?" I ask Austin as he drops me off at the hotel. Without hesitation he points his finger at a bar across the street. "Ask the bartender for a Category 5. Don't take more than two, and I'll see you in the morning."

I follow the script exactly, and an hour later find myself walking through the twilight to the lighthouse, through a world that feels like a Chuck Berry record played extra, extra slow. I stop to watch a group of college students playing croquet in the yard of a beachfront house, the glowing sun almost done setting behind them. They could be carved into the side of a Halloween pumpkin, their dark forms sharp against the last evening light. I take the long way home and start seeing things I have missed on earlier walks. On the beach adjacent to my hotel sits a massive old homemade pontoon boat that appears to have been dry moored for some time. A few saplings grow through the floorboards, and underneath is a storage area for firewood. It looks like it could easily have danced twenty back in the day, and maybe, on certain rare evenings, still does. I climb atop and kick my feet off the bow to watch the last light of evening drain off in the distance. The stars emerge one by one, and I do my best to keep a tally. It feels good to have no particular place to go.

III.

The next day Austin and I clamber into the boat of his friend and fellow guide, Kevin Morlock. Heading east to one of the farther-flung islands of the archipelago, we'll be testing the ancient angler's conviction that the farther one travels from home port, the greater one's chance of success. The long ride gives me plenty of time to scrutinize Kevin's carp flies. They are among the most beautiful and intricate ties I've ever seen in all my years of fly fishing, each one an intimate menagerie of pheasant feathers and rabbit fur and deer hair and turkey marabou, some light, some dark, some imitating gobies, some crayfish. Many are jointed, some even triple jointed. I pluck out a little serpentine thing barely two inches long and see that it in fact has four segments. This, if you don't tie flies, is on the higher end of the obsession scale, like a baker grinding their flour by hand with grain scythed at dawn.

Kevin kills the motor in a calm bay and clambers high up on the poling platform, from which he'll move the boat along more stealthily than any set of oars or trolling motor would allow. "Perfect conditions today," he says softly from his perch. "It's going to happen." Clad in a white that blends in like some ethereal camo against the bright, scudding clouds, every word feels oracular. And I, for one, believe.

I take up my position, strip out seventy feet of line, and prepare to apply the lessons of moving slowly and taking it all in from the prior day. I know the waves will saw the images below into fractals and fragments that I must piece together. I know the wind will raise a hypnotic shimmer that I must not be lulled by. No daydreaming today. Only slow and steady scanning. I want my badge of honor. I want my carp.

Today the fish are everywhere, alone and in pairs, in trios and larger pods, occasionally stopping to munch something on the bottom before cruising along. It occurs to me that this creature looks pretty darn at home for a species that originated in Asia and didn't set fin into North American waters before the 1880s. I don't think other transplants would have fared as well. It's hard to imagine a Siberian tiger skulking across the wood lots of the Midwest, napping in the tall corn, popping whitetails like bonbons.

It doesn't take long before Kevin spots a target.

"Two o'clock. Forty yards. Tailing fish."

The fish, all alone on a sand flat, nose down, tail up, glows like the only penny in a wishing well.

"I see it."

"A dinner plate," Kevin reminds me softly. "You've got to drop your fly on its dinner plate or it won't see it."

Today I do everything right, casting beyond the fish so that it doesn't startle when my weighted fly plunks down, stripping the fly back so it's right above the fish before letting it fall down through the water column. If my fly is on target, this carp will see it as a tiny shadow slowly dilating on the bottom, now the size of a pea, now a grape, now blooming into something very much worth looking up for—a succulent morsel of flesh parachuting down from the sky.

"Set!" Kevin cries.

I rear back to set the hook but only get halfway before the rod dives in the opposite direction and the carp takes off for the deep, splitting a pair of large boulders, bending the rod to the cork. I can understand now why Japanese samurais would carry carp-adorned paraphernalia as they headed into battle—this is a strong fish, evolved to surge over long distances and never tire.

Unlike the angler.

It takes a team effort, but finally we land the fish, which I admire quietly as it resuscitates in calm, knee-deep water. And it occurs to me that *carp* is just too sudden and stark a word for a creature that requires so much patience, so many overtures, such earnest effort of seduction. The Latin makes more sense, and also sounds good when whispered above the shush of the breakers. *Cyprinus carpio. Cyprinus carpio.* After a few moments my fish shakes its head and starts to fin its bulk across the flat, sweeping its large tail from side to side, gaining depth at its own pace, carving its way through the shimmering water at a deliberate but unrushed tempo.

Taking its sweet time, as any local would.

CHAPTER 12

Debonair Dirtbag

"YOU FLY ANGLERS ALL LOOK ALIKE." IF YOU FISH, YOU HEAR THIS all the time from nonanglers, who in addition to leading sorrowful lives, all have terrible eyesight. "My beard has gray flecks on the left side of my chin," I'll explain when one of these sad creatures wrongly tags me on social media. "Plus, my hat is digital camo, not analog. And if you zoom in, you can see that's a really aggressive weight-forward taper that guy's casting. Everyone knows I'm a long-belly kind of guy."

Then one day, while waiting out a flight at a tiny airport in Argentina, I finally got a taste of my own medicine. Amidst a hatch of traveling Patagonians drinking coffee and chatting sat a sole, pensive gringo. He was typing on the same laptop I had, which furthermore had the same stickers, but in a different configuration. The shirt he had on was also the same as mine—or was it that mine was the same as his? Our respective fates, too, I would soon learn, were mirror reflections of the other. Me: awaiting my return to the States to brag to friends about the huge Patagonian trout I'd just caught. Him: awaiting the arrival of clients from the States he would take to huge Patagonian trout.

I walked over, pointed at him, then me, then him again. "Me," I said, like Tarzan talking to Jane. "Me friend."

"You speak English?" he asked.

It turned out that his name was Justin Witt, a native Wisconsinite who'd been living in Argentina for the last decade, fishing and guiding the backcountry via a destination travel company he founded, one that featured all the best fishing Argentina had to offer, with none of the frills. In the time before my flight came, we talked about the fishing in Chile vs. Argentina, Jim Harrison vs. Tom McGuane, our favorite streamers, and whether there was any reason to visit Buenos Aires (there wasn't). When we parted, he shook my hand and said, "Come back some day and I'll take you into the backcountry. We'll catch a world-record brook trout. They're out there."

I get fishing invites fairly often, but this one I filed away in the "You Damn Well Better Do This" drawer, for six reasons. Reasons one to four were all variations of the same general idea: to catch giant brook trout. Reason five was because Justin was the closest I'd ever come to meeting my doppelgänger, and I knew from my previous life as a student of literature that very curious things happen when you roll with your 'ganger. The sixth and final reason was my curiosity about the type of program Justin runs down there, born of the egalitarian goal of providing guides and other working-class anglers the chance to experience ultra-fishy places without having to stay at ultra-spendy lodges—or lodges at all (we'd be living out of tents). This appealed to me greatly because it represented a world of experience I had never thought existed, a mythical middle realm sandwiched between what I like to think of as Camp Dirtbag and Camp Debonair—the two very different fishing worlds I tend to find myself in.

To clarify: Camp Dirtbag is where you and your friends pour over topo maps and satellite images for months, then bushwack deep into the Upper Peninsula or Ontario to spend a week portaging beaver dams and sleeping in swamps and tweezering ticks out of buttholes, all in the hope of finding the next brook trout or muskie Valhalla. Camp Debonair, on the other hand, is where some fancy lodge run by people who take showers every day do all the work for you; all you have to do is get off the plane, hand your luggage to a porter, and sip duty-free Wild Turkey while the switchbacks rock you to sleep.

Both modes of fishing have their perks. Camp Dirtbag is special because it offers the opportunity for the truest and most lasting type of fishing glory—because what greater angling accomplishment is there than solving a river's mysteries on your own? It's also got the right mix of pain and danger—there's just something about the threat of a cougar gutting you in your sleep like a wet burrito that makes the woods deeper, the night darker, and the trip more exhilarating. As if all that weren't enough, cooking and sleeping and fishing in nonstop rain for a week straight—which seems to happen more often than not at Camp Dirtbag—builds both character and *characters*. Very handy if you're a writer.

But it's also pretty nice over there in Camp Debonair, where the fishing is almost always good and occasionally mind-blowing. There, people you've never met before cook your food for you, and it appears on your plate magically and in heaping quantities every morning, noon, and night. When you fetch your waders in the morning, they're not frozen stiff as a shepherd's crook on a tree branch, but rather soft and warm and smelling of cedar from the sauna room. There's also very little danger of being maimed at Camp Debonair, since going home with a hook for a hand would be terrible for any outfit's Instagram feed. There are fishing programs for all manner of weather contingency, and no bodily harm accrues even after fishing all day in the nastiest stuff. Topped your waders and soaked your underlayers? Just place them next to your bedroom woodstove, and next morning they'll be warm as fresh-baked apple pie.

So those are the two great cosmic fishing realms, forever split asunder, never touching. But what if you could have the best of both? The pride and glory and freedom of Camp Dirtbag alongside the exotic vistas and excellent fishing of Camp Debonair? What would this Middle Kingdom look like?

This year the moons of Jupiter were all in a row, and come March I found myself visiting Justin and his friend Chris at Debonair Dirtbag headquarters—a simple house in Argentine Patagonia's Chubut Province in the town of Rio Pico. The home was owned by Justin's friend Paulino, aka "The Godfather," revered far and wide for his decades of fighting to protect the province's fish and fisheries from all manner of threat and exploitation. Out in the backyard, a butterflied lamb was brought sizzlingly to a table already wincing with Malbec, followed by steaming mounds of blood sausage and various offal. On an adjacent table, three mountains of onions, cilantro, and tomatoes stood at the ready. It had been a long time since my Miami airport corn dog, and as I filled my plate I wasn't just salivating, I was straight waterboarding myself.

At the end of the meal Justin called Chris and me over to a map he had spread open in the firelight. Our trip as planned would last nearly two weeks and consist of two parts: a week deep in the Andean bush to fish a remote river system, and a week exploring the high-country lakes. It was the first leg that I was most excited about. "You two are going to be part of a small handful of people who've ever fished these waters," Justin said, looking us very seriously in the eye. With a greasy rib bone he traced the route we'd take to the river in the morning. It entered the mountains as an old gaucho trail and proceeded to pass through several *estancia*s—sprawling, heavily forested cattle ranches. The drive into the bush would last two to four hours, depending on how many tributaries we'd be able to ford in the Hilux. Then we'd have a hike through rough country of between two and four hours, again depending on the conditions of the tributaries.

"This is my favorite place on Earth," Justin clarified as the last of the wine tinkled into my glass. This is saying quite a bit, since Justin has fished just about everywhere in the world, freshwater and salt, northern hemisphere and south, and he may be the only person in the history of the world to have eaten both boiled bear's feet (Kamchatka) and barbecued barracuda (Bahamas) in the same week. Nor does his life become less itinerant when he's not fishing. Between work trips he globe-trots in a tricked-out RV with a pretty Russian wife he met on a vision quest in the Peruvian jungle. Bumping along in the backseat is their daughter, the world's best-traveled one-year-old.

The next day we drove out of town, past mesas and mountains and horse-backed gauchos with their fleets of dusty dogs, all the while listening to a genre of music Justin described with a serious face as "Ojibway Square-dance." But below the music I noticed he was humming a very different tune. When I pressed him, he explained that it was something called an *icaro*, not exactly a song but rather a metaphysical laser beam of soundwaves designed to hack the universe at the molecular level—the shamans in the Peruvian jungle had taught him the art. Justin had *icaros* for all kinds of occasions—fording rivers, finding mushrooms, seducing giant brook trout. Whenever we mushed the Hilux through a particularly nasty mudflat, I noticed that his *icaro* got a little louder.

Finally we arrived at an unpassable crossing and disembarked. "We are now a three-hour hike from base camp," Justin said. Chris and I, being jacked up on the most dangerous kind of adrenaline, made the decision to chug a beer for every projected hour of the hike. It was a very bad idea. Not only is Justin fast, he's also offensively tall in a way I hadn't appreciated before—very unbecoming of a doppelgänger. Chris and I struggled to keep up with his loping gate as the forest kept closing in on him from either side. As a hiker I am decidedly not fast, hailing as I do from a long line of Polish and Ukrainian plodders, our genetics honed by centuries of chasing stray goats while nursing potato-spirit hangovers. But my people always got their goat, and Chris and I managed to keep Justin just close enough to avoid getting fatally lost in the Andean bush.

After what felt like forever we finally hit the river, located in a lush, densely wooded valley surrounded by low mountains covered in green stubble. Justin explained that farther downstream it would plummet through a series of towering waterfalls and high canyons, but the ten or so miles we'd be fishing were calm and smooth, with easy runs of softball-size stones and bright-green vegetation swaying in the pools. The solitude as we set up camp was immense. Twice I thought I heard human voices coming from deep in the forest, but it turned out to be a trick of the wind and trees and river—there was no one out here but our tribe of three. We made a fire, had dinner, and washed the plates not with camp soap and a Brillo pad but spongy lichens and fragrant herbs, which somehow still cut through the grease and left the plates smelling like orange and thyme. We drank with cupped hands straight from the river without the intermediary of a water filter, and as the night wore on, I started to feel less like a modern hominid and more like an ancient australopithecine, one of those creatures with bulging foreheads and bad haircuts from the pages of my college anthropology textbook. When finally I lay back in my sleeping bag, I decided that the development of human civilization had been a colossal waste of time. This was the only way to live.

The next morning we had a breakfast of bread, bacon, and oranges, then hiked upstream toward the headwaters. But when after an hour of forest walking we came to the edge of a cliff, I saw no river, just an expansive valley of reeds, hundreds of acres' worth, a continent of shoulder-high scallions. We followed Justin down into the marsh and started walking through the vegetation, presumably to the other side of the canyon. Then Justin stopped and pointed ahead of him. "Gentlemen, we have arrived," he said. There, glowing faintly blue through the reeds, invisible unless you were directly on top of it, was a narrow but deep channel of clear, cold water. I unslung my fly and made a short steeple cast.

"Fish," I said.

"Fish," Justin echoed, his trout breaking water upstream of mine.

"Fish," Chris said from down below.

The river was just as Justin promised, no fish under sixteen inches and quite a few just shy of twenty. In fact, my third fish of the day was the biggest brook trout I had ever seen in real life. "You'll catch one that big or bigger every day," Justin assured. The size of the fish was something my brain could not exactly compute. Here I was, throwing a 6-weight and articulated streamer at a species I typically dappled at with a 3-weight and bushy dry. I studied each fish that entered the net with a mix of awe and unease, stuck in an uncanny fontinalis valley. These could not be brook trout. Could these be brook trout? They couldn't. Could they? It wasn't until the end of that day, some ten large brook trout later, that I could release them without feeling unsettled, that I was sure they were fish and not fictions.

Each day we fished either upriver or down from base camp, pushing farther afield to access new water, lengthening our forays in both directions as our strength increased and our comfort with the terrain grew. This psychological component was important because the density of the brush challenged you not only physically, but mentally. Working your way through the understory felt like long division, only instead of holding the remainder in your head, you had to remember where you'd come from in case you ran into a wall of brambles or canyon and had to backtrack fifty yards. Several times a day I felt like a cat at the top of the proverbial tree, knowing that somehow I had gotten here but with no idea how to get back. Every evening I dabbed ointment on the bleeding lines of my arms.

By the third day I'd caught enough fish to have made a few observations about what to expect from any given pool. It seemed my best trout always came on the fifth or six fish out of a spot, with each fish being bigger than the one that came before, like a Russian doll in reverse. But at the hole where I would catch my largest trout, something else happened altogether. The day in question was a sunny one, which had us fishing a stretch of river that passed through a thick cedar forest. It was dark both in the woods and on the water, with only isolated columns of light falling here and there through the canopy. The river in this section was particularly tortuous, with sharp bends, deep holes, and undercut banks guarded by the gnarled roots of half-fallen cedars. I tied on a pattern I typically save for low-light conditions, an extra-large white Murdich Minnow with enough flash that I could see its glow with my eyes closed. Then around the next bend I came across as perfect a lie as I had ever seen.

A long, heavy tongue of current had gouged a hole in the gravel and cobble and cut a hard seam that ran past a large deadfall, a gnarly gargoyle of timber that looked like it might come alive to hunt gauchos on full-moon nights. Behind it, up against the bank, gyred a deep eddy. Below it, in the tailout, sat a pair of large boulders. As is my custom with promising spots, I spent a moment identifying how I'd fight a large fish and where I'd try to land it. Anything eating near the wood would have to be bullied out immediately—before the fish knew what hit it. After that, the only real danger was the faster water down below. Satisfied with my plan, I started fishing very deliberately. Fish one, two, and three followed the previous crescendoing pattern I'd identified, each about an inch bigger than the one before. But four, five, and six got smaller and smaller in rapid succession, and the seventh was the smallest fish I'd caught yet that week.

I scratched my head and rested the hole. Where was the pig? It was a prime lie in a world of prime lies, and yet here were small brook trout feeding fearlessly. Could it be my instincts were off and there was no behemoth around? I tapped my finger on the hook point and parsed the water again.

Whether somewhere beyond the trees Justin was humming an *icaro* is impossible to tell, but as the Murdich swung across the face of the logjam for the umpteenth time, it disappeared in a dark, muscular boil. I set the hook hard and my throat immediately constricted. It was an extremely large fish, and it had eaten right in the wood. It took all the 6-weight's backbone and all my fourteen-pound tippet's strength to win those first crucial seconds, but I did, putting the trout's weight on the butt of the rod and backing up into the current. Now, with the fish in open water, I needed a net man. Fast.

Since we were fishing well apart from each other and only had one net between the three of us, we had agreed to yell out the word *barraco*—Spanish for "fat one"—in case of a good fish. But in the heat of the moment, my brain short-circuited and instead I screamed out a similar-sounding Japanese word associated with splashing soup. It worked. Justin came tearing out of the brush and scooped the fish up with the net, then let out a whoop of exaltation at the size of the fish. I collapsed against the bank, relieved not to have lost the fight.

We stood there for some time marveling at the great fish's shoulders. After a decade of brook trout fishing, here was a specimen that could have eaten the largest brookie I'd ever caught in the U.S. and probably still had room for more. And though it was no native, in a way I felt like I was seeing the species for the first time. The difference was the size. Studying the markings of all my past Midwestern fish, I realized, had been like reading the tiny script on a medicine bottle. Here at my feet was *S. fontinalis* in extra-large font, a newspaper made for the elderly. Staring at this supremely legible specimen, I finally understood the species' markings, its camouflage. Those light olive etchings on that dark olive back, which some refer to as vermiculations but I'd always thought of as cuneiform, were actually sunlight through riffle water, trembling on stone bottom.

After a truly great fish there comes, for me at least, a pleasant loosening of the brain and body that changes the tenor of the trip. For one, it generally makes me a better angler since my nerves are no longer on edge, and I care a little less about angling outcomes. This makes my casts better and hook sets sounder. Secondly, since I'm a fishing writer, there's also less need for focused detail gathering after a great fish because I've already collected my primary set piece. Thus whatever happens in the hours—and sometimes days—after a great fish becomes, in memory at least, a creamy blur. And that's how I remember the rest of our brook trout trip, a soft bokeh of shadow and trees and mountaintops, all gooped in honeyed light. That is, until our sudden and dramatic departure.

The scene must be set. It was the night after what had been by far our longest day trip, during which we'd fished our way downstream to a large waterfall and hiked many miles of thick wood back. We were the kind of tired where you don't talk as you prepare and eat dinner. There was no discussion about the next day's fishing, no joking, no goodnights. Even farts took more energy than the body possessed and had to be saved for the following morning. But for some reason, as utterly exhausted as I was, when I crawled into my sleeping bag, I could not fall asleep.

The minutes became hours, two hours became four, and still I stood staring at the unblinking stars. Sleep was the thing I needed most, since tomorrow we would have our deepest hike yet, all the way up to the headwater lakes for one last shot at a world record, and I would need all possible strength. But no sleep came. I started to imagine each passing minute as a wolf that was eating into my store of future energy, bite by gulping bite. By 4am the wolf was getting bigger and bigger, while I was getting smaller and smaller. Soon there would be no me left.

Then, for the first time all week, it started to rain. I felt the first drops on my face and moved my sleeping bag back into the tent. The rain built to a soft, soporific patter, and I could finally feel sleep coming. The wolf whined at the door for a minute but eventually slinked away. *Three hours*, I told myself. *Three hours of sleep till breakfast.* It wasn't much, but it just might be enough to get me through the next day without injuring myself with a misstep.

Then the tent unzipped and Justin's voice boomed in my ear.

"Pack. Pack right now. The rivers are rising, and if we don't leave immediately we'll be trapped."

Thus did we begin our Death March, in the steady rain, in the sleepless dark, hour after hour, till my headlamp, much like the man wearing it, weakened to almost nothing. We had to backtrack three times, once due to a pair of take-no-shit skunks, the others due to the fact that not even Justin had made this hike out in the dark, and it was easy to get turned around. Every half hour we'd stop for a quick snuff break, which provided welcome short bursts of energy, but by the final leg of the trip the tin had gone empty. As we plodded onward toward a dawn that didn't seem to be coming, I started to feel the hot breath of the wolf behind me. He was back, stronger than ever. I fell to a knee. I prepared to expire.

Then ahead of me in the darkness came the roar of the Hilux, the most beautiful sound I'd ever heard. I stood up, gave the wolf the finger, and scampered inside. Faces covered in snuff mud, Justin, Chris, and I shared a moment of profound silence. The first week of our trip was over. We had fished hard and well. And survived. Ours was the glory. Great fish and biblical suffering are the two parts of a fishing trip that can never be forgotten. It's why I'll never give up Camp Dirtbag, even if I win the lottery someday, or write a bestseller: It gives you memories that no amount of money can buy.

"I know where we can get warm," Justin said as he eased the truck forward. "A fishing camp run by an old Russian with one kidney, one lung, and half a liver."

Chris asked, "Do they make old Russians any other way?"

An hour later we pulled up to a hobbity cottage in a forest clearing. Chris and I had to duck to enter; Justin bent almost down to the waist. The Russian in question was wearing a brown, tattered robe and slippers, and he looked to be at least 85 years old. In a surprisingly strong voice he introduced himself as Nikita, great grandson of Czar Nicholas II's personal doctor, then herded our shivering bodies toward the woodstove. From the next room I could hear the tinkling of shot glasses being gathered, and a moment later Nikita's daughter emerged with a bottle of homemade vodka, spiced with the long spears of local grasses. Hot tea was placed right next to my shot glass, which Nikita filled to puddling. Justin cut up a loaf of bread and laid it slice by slice on the woodstove. For the next hour the best toast I'd ever tasted in my life came in endless waves alongside butter, jam, honey, and ham. The vodka tasted like a summer meadow. The woodstove kept eating more wood. Shot glasses were emptied and shot glasses were filled. I did not ever want to leave.

But we did, of course. There was more fishing to be done. In a fishing life—which is the one thing my maybe not-so-doppelgänger doppelgänger and I most definitely share—there is always more fishing to be done. I drowsed in the backseat as we headed back to Paulino's, listening to Justin talk about all the lakes we'd fish over the next week, the deep, cold high-country lakes with only numbers for names. After a while the radio came on, but I knew by now to listen below the music and soon found what I wanted to hear. Just under the electric guitar and just above the rush of highway, Justin was humming an *icaro*. But it was a new one, with a different melody and a different pitch. What did this one do? Who was this one for?

Somewhere off in the distant mountains, in the lonely lakes where big trout sulk, the water started to quiver.

CHAPTER 13

Life of Chum

It's a good life, being a camp dog. Even better to be top dog at fish camp. And if you were on your best behavior in all your past lives, you might be reincarnated as the alpha canid at an Alaska salmon camp—as did a certain mutt named Chum.

I first met Chum as he prowled beneath the tables of the sprawling mess tent at Deneki's Alaska West camp on the Kanektok River, nose alert to the New York strip and king crab humped high on everyone's plate, waiting for a piece of gristle to drop, or a pincer to fall. He was small enough to creep under tables without detection, quiet enough to startle you in your tent when you turned around, and light enough to be carried like a boat bag into his owner's jet sled—his favorite place to be. Once onboard he clambered to the front deck where, with a small dog's obliviousness to size and station, he assumed the role of head scout. Nose to the wind as the jet shrieked upriver, Chum's dominion extended beyond the boat to all that lay ahead, the deep pools and gravel bars and thousands of fish in all stages of kype and color, including those whose name he bore.

Chum's was a rags-to-riches story of the first order. As a small pup not much bigger than a yam he was rescued from a dumpster by Alaska West guide Ryan Gossett, who noticed something squirming inside a garbage bag during one of his forays to the downriver town of Quinhagak.

The camp nursed the pup back to health, and Chum quickly established himself as a quiet, confident companion for camp guides, staff, and visitors alike. But camp dogs have duties beyond mere companionship. In these temporary settlements at the edge of the human world, they are also seers of sorts, privy to all those worlds invisible to the human eye: that griz a few yards deep in the brush as you fish out a side channel; the moose skulking beyond the tents during what passes for night in the subarctic summer; the waves of fresh fish coming in off the sea. This makes them mascots in the truest sense of the word. In its corrupt modern usage, the term is associated with bug-eyed buffoonery—the parrot falling over itself at a high school football game. In actuality, *mascot* comes from the Provençal word *mascotte*, meaning "lucky witch." There is no doubt Chum was lucky, and I'd like to think that his mojo rubbed off on the entire camp. Who can say how many forty-plus-inch kings his luck accounted for, how many sleeping lives were saved from bears, wolves, and evil northland spirits?

Chum worked his spell on all who came into contact with him, and his power extended well beyond his mortal form. His visage appears on the fish room whiteboard, on the wall of the latrine, in the photo albums of camp guests—honored in art just like his camp-dog ancestors who were chiseled into stone or painted onto cave walls. And just like those first domesticated half-wolves that came in from the woods at night to sleep beside the fire, camp dogs—like fly fishing itself—are at once a reminder of the wild world and an affirmation that we exist apart from it.

If Chum was aware of his limitations, he was also deeply disinterested in them. This ultimately led to his demise. Like the trapper who survives mountain lions and avalanches, only to be undone by an escalator in his first department store, Chum, while on sabbatical in Oregon last fall, succumbed to something he didn't see often in the bush: an automobile.

You could say that Chum's luck ran out. I'd prefer to say that his lucky spirit moved on to an even more charmed life, if there is such a thing after being top dog at fish camp.

CHAPTER 14

Into the Mystic

At 3am the second alarm goes and you rise up from your tying desk, put the last flies in the box, put the box in the dry bag, put yourself in the car. You leave it running in the street and dodge back inside, open the fridge to down the last of the meds you've come to call Pillzilla and wonder if this is the moment that will save you from—what did the nurse at the travel clinic call it . . . Delhi belly? It won't. At the airport check-in the clerk looks at you sideways, a child points and squeals, and the TSA agent pulls not one but two yellow Schlappen feathers out of your hair. His unamused *what is this?* confirms not everyone is flying halfway around the world to chase a fish whose name they may or may not know how to pronounce.

Detroit to Boston, Boston to Dubai, Dubai to Delhi. Not miles and time zones but thresholds and wonderment. Perfect desert cities laid out like craps tables, yachts flecked across square blue bays. Calls to prayer circling like birds in the light-soaked airport terminal. The extra-planetary ridges of Pakistan's high country, brutal and inscrutable in low sun. The VHS haze of downtown Delhi.

At a hotel bar in the North Indian town of Pantnagar, where you aim bullet after whiskey bullet at your jet lag's iron heart, a Sikh businessman asks what a mahseer is. You have no clue, you tell him, you've made very sure of that. The colonial-era English language books, the web discussion boards, the friends of friends who'd fished these rivers—you've avoided them all. Why eat of the tree of mahseer knowledge? Why touch its fruit? When ungodly portions of your life are spent divining the ways of fish, why go and ruin a perfect mystery?

"Leopards this side," the driver says as your late-model sedan courses north into mountains, a Pelican case on your lap, a temple of dry bags lashed to the roof. You're so jet-lagged your brain can't categorize what it's seeing, throws it all in your skull's junk drawer for future parsing: the first hundred monkeys, the wedding convoys garlanded in orange carnations, the pyramids of melons, all sizes, all colors; the second hundred monkeys, the stooped farmers shouldering blimps of rice, the cooking fires just inches from the highway, the motorbikes with whole families fused atop, young mothers riding sidesaddle with infants in their arms; the psychedelic trucks with their bright flags and ribbons and wreaths and painted-on license plates (some have brake lights, some don't); the third and fourth hundred monkeys, the heaps of sugarcane beside sweating vendors and their fresh sweet drinks, and all the vans with their back doors removed to carry a few more passengers, who clutch the roof and, with feet half on the bumper, stare down at the highway shrieking by. You feel a sudden and overpowering psychological dependence on the sari, the impossibly bright, unwrinkled, unblemished sari, which in this unsettled place of dust and smoke seems the only thing complete, finished, clean.

"Anyone ever catch a mahseer?" Georgetown John asks. You shake your head as much as motion sickness allows. New York Jon says no, but he has caught tigerfish and is just off the plane from Tanzania, where half his party left early after failing to keep their insides inside, their camp being located downwind from a buffalo slaughterhouse. "They missed some pretty good fishing, though." His partner, Tonya, has just one fishing trip under her belt, a bonefish trip the month prior. She's still looking for her first fish. You are looking for specimen 72,489. Yeah, you're counting.

At some point during this waking dream of color, dust, and switchbacks, you rest your eyes, and when you open them again it's dark. The car has stopped. The air is still. Before you can remember where you are, the door opens and someone in a headlamp hands you a trekking pole. John and Jon and Tonya huddle in the dark on the edge of something—a cliff? A flashlight shepherds you down a steep embankment to where shushing roar and riffling moonlight and earthy wet myrrh tell you incontrovertibly: Below is a river. It is the first familiar moment, this meeting new water in the dark, since your Detroit Bloody Mary fifty hours ago. As a Cataraft ferries your party across in silence you think of other night encounters: the West Fork of the Kickapoo, all manure and mint and starlight in slow pools; the Pere Marquette, that freakish warm winter night you listened in the dark fog to the snow tearing from the banks; the North Branch of the Au Sable boiling with trout during a midnight spinner fall; and now the Saryu and its bright beach bonfire and white-linened tables floating above the sand. The Saryu, with its dahl and goat dumplings and butter chicken and rice and naan steaming under silver domes. And you realize, though, you are not exactly sure where you are: This is a good place to be.

On the way to the temple the next morning your host delivers a crash course in Himalayan fishing, and it's the fullest attention you've given to human speech in months if not years. You realize you've been pronouncing it wrong, that it's not an iamb but a trochee: MAH-seer, an extra-sharp spiking of the first syllable, as if the word were ascending and descending one of the mountains surrounding you, sudden surge, soft fall. The mahseer, you learn, is a product of the monsoon, skilled in surviving when the river swallows the treetops and the boulders tonk so loudly you can hear them in your chest. "This is why the mahseer has such a sensitive lateral line and large, strong plates for scales," your host explains. "He dodges the rocks and boulders the river throws his way. And when he cannot dodge, he deflects."

You climb higher up the mountainside, past men herding goats and women with their sickles and scalpings of grass and red-and-yellow prayer flags tied to low trees. From the temple's porch you look through a stone arch down at the river and see huge mahseer bodies crammed into tailouts. Your host tells you of a Nepalese man with a gill net and float tube that snagged a mahseer so large it towed him hundreds of meters upriver, plowing a deep furrow in the water, swinging him this way and that before finally the man's hands pulped open and he released and kicked back to shore.

Inside the temple courtyard the holy man, Baba, is squatting in a pool of his own gray dreadlocks, jabbing wires into a dusty box until it wheezes tinny flutes. After *namastes* he enters a sacred area of burning coals and ash and sand and bells engirdled in the letters of a language so old that no one, not even Baba, can read them. You are blessed quickly and silently in the middle of your forehead and then given back to the afternoon, and you can still feel the thudding of Baba's ashen thumb an hour later, when from a riffle on the far bank, you swing up your first mahseer, a small but good thing with wide-set eyes and golden scales. The Mahakali fish are silver, your host tells you. Tomorrow you are going there, to the big, turbid, cold glacial water of the Mahakali, the river of the goddess of time and death.

The next morning you spend hours loading the rafts: There are boxes of live chickens and crates of cucumbers, melons, and onions. There are tents, latrines, and canopies; linens and tables and chairs; vats of spices and ghee; a large barrel of water; a small barrel of rice. As you put on your life jacket and helmet, a crew member suddenly too ill to make the trip asks to see your fly box. Then he rubs his fingers as they hover and pluck, hover and pluck, wadding a mess of fur and feathers into one corner. "In Chukka," he says, pointing at the flies he has sequestered. "Fish all these at the confluence in Chukka."

You nod. Chukka. A good fish will happen in Chukka. Basic metaphysics require it. A good fish is the salt that flavors everything that comes before it and after it, gives the trip dimension. A good fish is the spine that holds the story together, a center for memory. And in a strange place far from home, a good fish is the only way you can truly enter this world, to not simply bear witness to it but to partake of it. Because you do not play the drums or flutes, do not herd the goats, do not stoke the sacred fires, do not speak the language, do not kill the chickens, do not scalp the grass. There is only one port of entry by which you may enter into this world: a good mahseer. And, if it is a truly good mahseer, it may even become an eternal portal, granting passage back in time whenever you take a slow breath and close your eyes.

After two days of paddling, the river valley widens and signs of village life appear. Gaunt buffalo stagger over river cobble. Mango groves wizen, thirsty for rain. There are signs of mahseer life too. High up on boulders, like cave paintings or petroglyphs, lateral streaks mark where last year's monsoon fish gummed food off from rock. But there is a problem. Just a mile upstream from Chukka you encounter a rapids too dangerous to be crossed. The gear, food, and rafts themselves must be portaged, a job so big you must enlist the help of the villagers who turn out in flip-flops to carry your small fishing universe piecemeal across the cobbled floodplain, toward a distant tree line blurred with heat. They laugh as they work. Portage money is good money. And life in Chukka is hard. Your host explains that, because the surrounding villages have all been abandoned, more wildlife is returning, and the villagers do not welcome this. One speaks of having lost two buffalo to tigers this year, and the government only paid him for one. Another complains he can no longer plant potatoes or banana trees; the wild boar root out one and girdle the other. But then he smiles beneath a heavy pack and points at the sky. When the monsoon comes, he and his friends will throw fifteen rods out into the night, and in the morning, they will have fifteen big mahseer.

Halfway to camp you stop along a small clear stream, take off your boots and socks, and plunge your swollen feet in. The whole river flinches with sculpins, more than you've ever seen. You follow the stream down toward the confluence, watching the dark, furtive forms shuffle with each step, and where the cobble turns to sand, you come across a pile of ash, a flip-flop, a puddle of red, tattered cloth, and a curved shard of white that stands out among the smooth river rock. That shard. You back up and see the pile of ash stretches many feet in the other direction. You are not looking at something but someone, a person still remembered in bits and scraps through the ashes. You think of that word, *remains*. That which the fire did not get, that which the insects and wind did not get. Remains. You back away silently, leaving this person to wait for the monsoon in peace. Back at the camp you open your fly box and finally look to see what the guide at the Saryu camp had chosen for you: sculpins, every single one.

The days take on a cadence: eat, sleep, fish, rest, fish, rest, eat, fish, sleep. In Chukka, life is scripted by the heat. You've known heat in the Midwest, it seeps out of coffee cups, wobbles off blacktop, but it is small and neat and fixed. Here in Chukka on the Mahakali, the heat is everywhere and insistent, it finds a way into you, pushing off the white cotton sheets during midday siestas, a heat so hot it seems to stop time. It's better, you find, to skip naps, skip siestas, sit in the river up to your waist. And fish.

The first day goes by without a good fish, the second sees two fish taken, but they are still not what you're looking for. Then on the third day, the river you've been listening to deafly starts to speak in a voice you can hear. On a distant downstream beat, a few hundred yards from where a Jim Corbett bullet once split some wicked maneater's heart, from on top of a boulder overlooking a swift, gouging run, you spot a perfect greasy slick. Just the right size, just the right place, just the right speed. For half an hour you sample boulders for position. This one's too close for a good swing, this one's too far. But over here's a small, wet perch that, if you're careful not to slip, will be just right. You give it your best cast and start swinging, through the heaviest churning water first, then down across a slower edge, and just as your line straightens out your rod bucks, your reel screams, your empty hands tilt to fullness.

If while fighting this fish you could think, which of course you can't, you'd consider how strange and surreal it is to be battling a fish as strong and tireless as a steelhead while a hot wind wicks into your eyes; how raw your yelling-for-the-camera voice sounds from breathing the smoke of the pre-monsoon fires; how odd the sun looks in the noon sky, dark as an egg yolk behind a vellum of haze and heat, so dull you can look straight into it; how cold the water feels, having slid off the underbelly of a Tibetan glacier just a few days ago, even newer to this land than you are. These are the things you will think about, meditate about, much, much later. Right now there is only one thought, one question, over and over and over again: Can you keep this fish above the rapids?

You can. You do. After what feels like eons, you hold this perfect fish in a quiet cut behind a boulder, the way you rest brook trout behind your boots in Wisconsin, or rock muskies back to life among lily pads in the Upper Peninsula. The fish's stripe looks like some priest has thumbed it with a streak of ash. It reminds you of a bass. But it is not a bass. It isn't anything you know or could ever know, its strangeness only growing in your hands, the same plated scales that deflect the monsoon boulders now deflecting your understanding. No matter. It's coming back to life now, and as you turn it toward the current, you can feel through its armor both the strength that is and the strength that will be, on that future day when the high waters come and you are gone from this place, vanished save through this memory, which will flash and fade, flash and fade like the silver tail scything away from you, pushing back toward that mystic place in the cold, dark water that not even the mountains know.

CHAPTER 15

Catching on the Kanektok

WALRUS HAVE A PENIS BONE CALLED AN OOSIK—LIGHTER IN HAND than a moose foreleg, it makes an excellent salmon bonk. Black bear bile can heal your liver and melt your gallstones—and get you arrested if you're caught in possession. If you are encircled by grizzlies and need to cross homicidal CFS to safety, doff your waders, trap them with air, and float to the far bank—but kiss your boots goodbye. Mullets are the most utilitarian haircut known to man—only the word is pronounced *moo-LAY*.

In an essential place, one learns essential things.

This July afternoon I am indeed in such an essential place—western Alaska's Kanektok River. More precisely, I'm up to my waist in a chum salmon pool fighting my fifth fish in as many casts, this one raging like it's just snorted a full tub of bath salts. This particular specimen has me feeling less like an angler than a matador (my buddy's warning to wear a cup on the Kanektok was not wrong), and after charging me twice it turns on a dime and takes off in the direction of the Bering Sea. My fishing mates, Hillari Denny and Doc Rideout, groan impatiently. Though we've only been at it a few hours we've already learned that one angler tethered to a fresh chum is danger, two is a cat's cradle, and three is a broken-rodded bird's nest, and thus have adopted a policy of casting into the chum pool one at a time. It is, after all, only the first day of a weeklong trip, and we need to keep all remaining 7-weights intact.

"Must be foul hooked," I shout, and right on cue the fish breaches to flaunt a hook stuck squarely in its mouth. My guide chortles. Hillari and Doc shake their heads. I crank the knob on my drag and look for a similar mechanism on my arm.

The signs this would be a special trip were there the moment we debarked the plane in Quinhagak, a coastal village on western Alaska's Kuskokwim Bay, just south of the Yukon Delta. Our airport-to-lodge shuttle was the most impressive fish ride I'd ever seen, a refurbished school bus with its rear cab stripped to create a room-size gear bed where the eighth graders would have sat. On the ride out we saw a gross ubiquity of fish in every stage of life and death—leaping out of the river to shake sea lice, dangling from the eaves of the natives' smokehouses, hanging in the mouths of raptors and gulls. Then there was our pole-and-tarp digs. There's just something about a tent camp that speaks to the seriousness of the piscatorial endeavor. Many of my best fishing days have started with me staring up at a pitched tent ceiling in the dark, grasping around for my headlamp, wondering where the heck I am.

Finally the chum comes in, and there is much rejoicing. It's a big chrome male with sea lice for days, which earns it a bonk and free ride to the smokehouse. Hillari is up next and in no time she's rearing back into a popper-eater that makes her reel sing like a stuck pig. I watch it thrash and tail-walk as I pick a gnarly bowtie out of my running line, unaware that my own fly has slipped off its guide and is dangling in the water ten feet away. Suddenly a big chum slams it like a cheater's first move in tug-of-war, and I barely free my digits before the knot squeaks tight and the fish rips downstream.

That's another essential thing I've learned today: You can lose a finger on this river if you're not careful.

﹘﹖

At seventy-five miles long from its birth high among the glaciers in the Ahklun Mountains to its eventual embrace of the Bering Sea, the Kanektok is a small, even intimate, river by Alaskan standards—the two rivers just to the north, the Kuskokwim and the Yukon, are seven hundred and two thousand miles long, respectively. But what the Kanektok lacks in length it makes up for in diversity of character. In a few days an angler can float from the cold headwaters—*kanektok* is the Yup'ik word for "snowy"—all the way to the flat, alluvial marsh of Quinhagak—Yup'ik for "new formed river channel." Indeed, new channels are muscled out from the Kanektok's spring torsions every year, and a view of the middle river from above looks positively helical, a glittering DNA strand of water latticed by bear trails. From June to September, its banks are as close to the center of the salmon universe as you can get without sprouting gills. Kings run mid-June to mid-July, chums mid-June to mid-August. Sockeye appear in late June and do their thing until the end of the next month. Every other year, pink salmon patrol the river from mid-July to early August. Bringing up the rear of the salmon train, silvers run late July through mid-September.

But the Kanektok is a conveyor belt of a different sort too, hosting an annual angler migration that is global in its reach. Most of my Alaska expeditions are filled exclusively with Americans, but the Kanektok sees a strong early summer run of Europeans, who make up at least a third of our party of twenty. The draw is the legendary king salmon fishery. While there is good king fishing down the western coast of North America, there are only a few places where you are likely to land a face cord of chinook a week—what counts as an excellent outing when the Kanektok run is at its peak. I've timed my trip on the downslope of the king run, mine a gambler's game where I'll wager numbers of fish for specimens of tremendous size: The last few fish to come in from sea are the biggest.

There are many challenges to western Alaska king fishing. The first is abiding by the cadence of the tides. On my swing water back in Michigan the daily CFS has more fixity than the stars, but the best king water on the lower Kanektok heaves and falls to the tune of fifteen feet a day. This requires anglers to use their line hand to manage the speed of the swing as a morning progresses. As the tide comes, the current slows, a pure swing is amended by a steady left-hand stitch, and before you know it you're bringing the fly back in long, slow strips, like some grandmother working her triceps at the gym. Then there's the importance of being alert and using your eyes. Down in the distance, between the old moose skeleton and the abandoned snow machine, you'll see a pod of fish breach, at which point you must throw down your sandwich or coffee or camera and make sure your fly is swimming as the pod passes—just don't swing your offering too low, since the tidal bottoms are rife with silt and kings like to swim with their chins above the murk. Finally, if you are lucky enough to get bit, the king salmon hookset asks you to be Buddha and beast at the same time, letting the fish calmly eat the fly and turn downstream, then driving the hook home with a pneumatic intensity—what the guides call *crossing the eyes.*

After which, best of luck.

The Kanektok has its year-round residents as well, rainbows and grayling and Dolly Varden that spend the summer playing Pacific salmon bumper car but are rewarded with endless fatty eggs in return. Given all this variegated fishing opportunity, Kanektok days are predictable only in their unpredictability. You might start the day swinging kings with the big sticks before the current stalls and you hop in the boat to work the pinch points with a single-handed rod. After lunch on the bank, a chum tows you up a side channel where big rainbows with junkyard dog genetics are sulking in a deep pool, chunks of flesh the size of Crunch bars in their maws. Casting at these fish percolates a *mykiss* jones, so you shoot upriver to mouse the afternoon away, working the logjams for rainbows that chomp in the wake of your mouse like Pac-Man. Then another boat whooshes by, a guide traces a wavelength in the air with his free hand—*the tide is going back out*—so you gun it back downstream to where the river meets the sea for one more shot at Leviathan.

In short, one thing leads to another.

One of our *how-did-we-get-here?* excursions finds us twenty miles upstream of camp egging a side-channel plunge pool where the dollies seethe like mosquito larvae in a storm puddle. After having a mostly quiet morning, Doc Rideout unleashes a one-man charmageddon, catching one cartwheeling dollie after another. I ditch my rod and instead focus on photography for a bit. I am, after all, paying for this experience with my camera and pen. I try and fail to capture some aerial acrobatics—the shutter keeps tripping too early or too late—before resorting to a few close-up studies. As I shoot, I pay particular attention to the species' metallic green cheeks and sides, which remind me of the fake grass in the Easter baskets I got as a kid. I admire the candy-pink spots, the way their snouts flush orange as if just starting to rust. And while I get a few decent images, I'm feeling more keenly than usual the limitations of the camera. The modern angler lives in an era of the photograph—we swipe, scroll, and tap more fish pics in a day than the previous generation used to see in a year. But I remain convinced that what fishing needs is not more photographs but more sounds, not an Instagram but a Piscaphone. To hear the sizzle of the drag, the stumbling of the angler on cobble, the collective sucking in of breath when a good fish jumps, and the guide sloshing forward to stab the net. To behold the hoots, hollers, and high-fives, and then, finally, to take in the awed silence that attends a fish's return to water. I take a few long-distance establishing shots to finish up the set, then case up the camera and return to the sweet, unpredictable, virtuosic music of fishing.

My best king happens midweek, for which I am grateful. No hired storyteller wants to worry about the business end of things as the fish clock ticks down to zero on the last day of a trip, or—worse—have to fashion a narrative around the old Thoreauvian bromide about fishing not being about the fish (I suspect the man was a bobber watcher who never caught anything of size). The hook-up happens on my twentieth—or is it two hundredth?—cast at a spot the guides call "Church Bells," since you can see the crude wooden belltower of the Saint Juvenaly Mission on the far bank. And it falls into the category of "pure luck." I'm moving forward out of my D-Loop when I see a large porpoising directly downstream of the water I'm aiming for. It's a breach in three parts—first head, then back, then tail—and looks like a big brown trout sipping a Hendrickson spinner back home in Michigan, if brown trout grew to forty inches. I'm too deep into my casting sequence to make any changes—what will be will be—but fate lays my fly down just ahead of the fish's approaching nose. The tug comes instantly, before the fly has had a chance to sink or swing. I set the hook and the fish rockets out of the water in my exact direction before taking off downstream.

Way downstream.

When an angler already suffering acute salmonitis in his biceps, wrists, and obliques first hooks up with a king salmon fresh from the sea, it's unclear who is going to emerge the victor. The first few minutes of the fight are a blur. And then, slowly, I start to gain ground.

That's when the anxiety sets it.

I know I have a good fish on when I begin to fear—really and truly fear—losing it. On one hand, it is a silly, unaccountable feeling. Nothing material hangs in the existential balance; I have no personal history of hunger or hardship. On the other hand, the fear is real, palpable—my throat constricts, my heart flutters, my stomach turns on its side. I suspect this response is due to some collective human memory of scarcity and the danger it represents. *This is a fish that will make a difference*, some ancient part of the brain recognizes, remembering a dark time when the difference between life and death was a few extra pounds of flesh. The grimness with which I battle great fish expresses itself in other ways too. Followers of my future Piscaphone account will easily distinguish between tiny and tremendous fish. Catching dinks, I laugh through an open smile. Wrestling giants, I curse through gritted teeth.

After ten more minutes—enough time for me to exhaust my personal encyclopedia of profanity—my guide motions that *it is time*. I do as I have been instructed all week, keeping the fish in waist-deep water (shallow water freaks them out) and lifting its head just as the net harpoons forward. My jaw unclenches. My heart relaxes. Deep within my skull a few synapses in my brain stem sizzle: *We shall survive this long winter yet.*

We all take turns staring at the fish's bulk up close. It's forty inches of chrome with a faint magenta hue, with a great forked tail at one end and a gaping black maw at the other. We take a few pictures, and when it's time to say goodbye, I find a quiet, unmuddied spot for the release. In those last moments before letting the fish go, a familiar melancholy settles in, a feeling I've never been quite able to explain. It only happens with the very best fish, those dreamy beasts for which you devote long hours at the vise and push yourself through more airports than is reasonable in a single day. Such fish function as a great and powerful fantasy—until you find yourself knee-deep in water holding one by the tail. And then it is as if this great being, this finned myth, this scaled god has fallen pitifully out of the sky in the middle of an earthly day, and you are standing there watching its bent wings twitch and flounder. There's a sense of deep vulnerability in this moment, an awareness that if this impossible dream is real and mortal, then you, who are far less impossible, are real and mortal too.

Dusk is coming in purple and the river streams silver when my best king salmon swims off.

There's a feeling, in the endless twilight of an Alaska summer night, of having wandered into some fashion of afterlife. You glut on king crab and strip steaks and salmon cooked three ways, then stroll back down to the river for just a few more casts before bed, which turn into a few more hours of casting. There's something different about this extra round of fishing, when the light genuflects and the moon rises above the alders into a not-quite-night-sky. It feels quieter, more intimate, existing apart from the everyday business of fishing. Other spirits mill about. A native from Quinhagak arrives on an ATV to meditatively cast a spoon. A few guides slip away to egg rainbows in the permadusk. Ted Leeson once wrote that modern angling was born when certain of our ancestors, after netting and trapping and cleaning fish all day, snuck back to the water at night with a stick and string, because they just could not stay away. Evenings on the Kanektok corroborates this theory, and no time more so than on the last night, when even those guests who usually go to bed after dinner find themselves waddling out to the beach and taking up a position in the run. A few guides assemble a bonfire on the beach, giving the blue mercury of the river a golden glow. Bear stories begin to circulate. One of the guides walks around with an electric hair trimmer giving away free mullets. There are two takers. At the edge of the fire, Chum the camp dog rests with his chin on his paws, ears trained toward the darkening trees and what might lay beyond.

Among the guests, talk turns to naming our respective highlights of the week. Answers are predictable. "My forty-pound king." "When that twenty-eight-inch rainbow crushed my mouse." "The day I caught a hundred pounds of fish without moving my feet." But when it's time for one of the older Brits to answer, he just shakes his head and smiles. "All of it," he says. "I just like catching."

I just like catching. Catching. The intransitive act. No object. I've never heard the phrase, can't tell if it's rare poetry or a British commonplace, but its purity makes my head ring like a bell. Serious anglers who devote their lives to the rod fall can fall prey to a connoisseurship at odds with the simplicity that first seduced us. They start saying things like, "I only fish topwaters" or "Life is too short for nymphing." I once saw a homemade bumper sticker that read, "Tricos or GTFO." I repeat that phrase, "I just like catching," and think, *That is exactly right.*

Before heading to my tent I walk down to the water one last time. I pick up my 8-weight and take up position in the middle of a run between a pile of driftwood and some old grizzly tracks. I'm just here to catch, I tell the river—no objective, no expectation. I make one last cast after another, on this perfect summer night, under a perfect twilit sky, in what feels like the very center of the world.

CHAPTER 16

Now I Lay Me

I had different ways of occupying myself while I lay awake. I would think of a trout stream I had fished along when I was a boy and fish its whole length very carefully in my mind; fishing very carefully under all the logs, all the turns of the bank, the deep holes and the clear shallow stretches, sometimes catching trout and sometimes losing them. I would stop fishing at noon to eat my lunch; sometimes on a log over the stream; sometimes on a high bank under a tree, and I always ate my lunch very slowly and watched the stream below me while I ate.

—ERNEST HEMINGWAY, *THE NICK ADAMS STORIES*

I.

In my sleeping bag on the east slope of the Andes, a few yards from what might be the best brook trout river in the world, I was staring up at the stars and feeling strange. Why I could not say. The weather was perfect, there were no mosquitoes, and every so often a cool breeze swept in off the mountains to stoke the dwindling campfire—a scene straight out of an angler's lullaby. From my campmates came the gentle seesaw murmur of easy sleep, but not from me. I just squirmed there in my sleeping bag on a crush of ferns, heart trotting and brain glowing, watching the last sparks curl up into the stars.

I was at this time in my mid-30s and square in a rash of years when my life was fishing and my fishing was travel. My packs and bags rarely left the staging area of my bedroom floor; the only thing that changed was what went into them. Wet-wading boots and malaria pills for India. A box of foam dragonflies for Chile. Black-fly prophylactics for Labrador. A canoe paddle and fillet knife for Manitoba. Always a Moleskine, always a Fischer Space Pen, always a

Pelican case chock full of camera gear. In this way I traded words for water, often fishing alongside people who made more in a week than I did in a year. At least once a trip one of these elder gentlemen would pull me aside and ask, mistaking access for affluence, how I had gotten the best job in the world.

My non-fishing life was a different story. There I was an adjunct writing teacher in a bad economy and subject to all the glories that came with that station. I did my laundry with quarters, held my Jeep together with duct tape and zip ties, and rented a month-to-month room in a house with such a lopsided tenant-to-bathroom ratio that I was active in the chamber-pot lifestyle. I had no savings or retirement, only a good heap of credit card debt that I would float until my tax refunds hit and it was time to open the new fly-tying catalogue and start mounding next year's debt.

But none of that mattered while the opportunity to catch beautiful fish in gorgeous environments persisted. So while my friends were getting married, buying houses, and having kids, I was out in Nepal slaloming through my own vomit trying to catch a great mahseer, or mountain biking game trails to access secret Ontario brook trout lakes, or sitting in post-Soviet fish-and-game offices, counting out bribe money. And while the best I ever did financially was break even on these trips, I did come back very much in the black when it came to stories—about close calls with grizzlies; about the guide who insisted on using Raid in place of DEET and was no more; about the Alaskan bush pilot who saw the devil in the air and never flew again. I was full, too, of strange knowledge. I knew the altitude from which a Beluga whale looked like a grain of rice. I knew that, if you waded slowly enough on the shorelines of Manitoba lakes, the pike would hunt you.

But now, a few days into my third trip to Patagonia in as many years, with a group of people I had never met before and would probably never see again, I felt deeply homesick for the Midwest. I wanted to smell white pine, to hear the whine of mosquitoes, to feel the soft sand shifting beneath my boots in strong flow. I wanted to watch the pot boil and see the first *Hexagenia limbata* of the year. I wanted to be there when the last tricos fell.

Sleepless and nostalgic, I decided to do my best Nick Adams and get to work on those rivers I knew best. I waded up the Tomorrow and fished the hole below the old train trestle and caught two good fish, but when I tried to push farther downstream, I realized that I could not remember what came next, so I had to push back up through the water I'd just fished, and caught nothing the second time around. Then I slipped into the Pine River at Little Cambodia and caught a few nice brook trout before coming up upon the culvert at the county-line road. I made a cut across the woods to get above the impounded water but just found myself looping around and around in the swamp, having forgotten the location of the great fallen cedar that bridges over the impassable muck. Finally I tried Rulland's Coulee, gently raising the barbed wire and crawling on my belly through the cow pasture, but I could not remember which way the river bent as you made your way upstream or down, so I just fished the pool by the access over and over again. I caught two smaller fish, then hooked into a larger trout that split my legs downstream and disappeared. I tried my best to follow but stumbled into nothing but fog.

I tried harder, searching deeper back through water I used to know like the back of my hand—the Menominee where the Peme Bom Won comes in, the Manistee above Cameron Bridge Road. But it was no use. In place of memories of rivers I knew well, or thought I knew well, there were only bits and snatches of more recent travels. A king salmon porpoising on the small water of the Upper Togiak. A brown trout slashing across the blue water of the Futaleufú. A tight pod of mahseer pooled up where the Saryu meets the Mahakali. One could spend an entire life this way, I thought, fishing great rivers in beautiful parts of the world and never fishing one twice. One could grow old bouncing between continents and hemispheres, never knowing a single body of water well.

By now the eastern sky was growing pale and the early risers were making coffee. I crawled out of my bag, cleared my throat, and practiced my smiling, hoping no one would discover my great secret—that the adventuring angler who had lain down with them had been swapped out in the night by something else entirely: a man with a desperate need for a trout camp.

II.

There are several ways to come into a place on the water. By far the best is to inherit one, which is also the only way to gain triple-digit acreage and a vintage, first-growth log cabin, but that was impossible for a first-generation American like myself. Marrying into property is another excellent and proven path, but my commitment issues made that the mootest of moot points. Then there was the puritanical passage of working hard, making wise decisions, and sacrificing id-driven impulse for the long-term reward of a comfortable cottage on a fishy bend. But waiting that long meant the reward would also come with a set of bifocals, a trick shoulder, and possibly a set of titanium knees, and I didn't want to wait until I has half android before posting up on my own piece of paradise. I would have to find another way.

Back home in Ann Arbor, however, as I sat in front of my laptop and scrolled through real estate listings for vacant land in Northern Michigan, I had no idea what that other way might be. And yet I searched. That first year of looking for a place of my own was full of absurd obsessions. Three hundred acres with a mile of frontage on the Ontonagon if I finished the novel I abandoned in grad school *and* sold the film rights. Jim Harrison's old place outside Grand Marais if I could get a bunch of friends to go in on it (I tried, I failed). There were six months when I couldn't stop talking about a relatively cheap eight-hundred-acre tract in the Upper Peninsula with several branches of the Fox River flowing through it.

"You could plant one potato per acre," I told friends as we drank porch beers and watched the tenured professors we would never be walk to their cars. "One potato. And you'd *still* have enough potatoes to last the year. *Even if you ate two a day.*"

But it was all just fantasy, I was reminded every time I looked at my checking account, which was tethered to a "no minimum" savings account that had held four dollars in it since August 2005. And so I did what a writer does: I got to writing extra hard. I sold two fishing books and a half-dozen fly rods. I paid down some credit card balances. I posted Craigslist ads for all nonessential camping and fishing items. And when I found a place I thought was in my wheelhouse—a vacant sixteen-acre parcel on a river I had fished often back in the day—I headed over to the bank to see what sort of financing I qualified for. My pre-approval number left me wide-eyed and shell-shocked. It barely—and I mean barely—required a comma.

With no change in my financial situation in sight, I forced myself to admit that a place of my own would never happen. And so I refocused on travel and got back on the road. I fished arctic Quebec for Atlantic salmon, made my third trip to Bristol Bay, traveled by train across the Ontario wilderness. I doubled down on the fire-and-ice lifestyle of a traveling outdoor writer, one week having Scotch and cigars with guys who shared antique gun refurbishers with Hollywood celebrities, the next tiptoeing through midnight hallways with piss-filled mason jars in each hand. And then, one day, everything changed.

❧

On the day I encountered the stream of enchantment I was on a tour of small-stream restoration projects in Northern Michigan in order to write a story that would bring awareness to a federal funding initiative soon to expire. It was an assignment outside my typical writerly wheelhouse, which in mode and manner was generally closer to carnival than conservation. Bodily, I was very present. Mentally, I was not all there. As we rumbled along through the emerald pine forest, occasionally pulling into the ferns to let a logging truck rumble past, I wasn't thinking about Michigan, the Midwest, or even the continental forty-eight. Instead, I was going over a mental checklist for an upcoming trip to Newfoundland. I had to get the sensor of my DSLR cleaned. I needed a new external hard drive. Refills for my Fischer Space Pen. Two more Moleskines.

But as we drove deeper into the woods—hoping the car didn't get stuck in a lake of dry sand, stopping at intervals to check the map—I began to remember the charms of an earlier fishing stage of my life, when I would escape to these smallest of small streams to be completely free and alone in the world. Seeing nothing but animal tracks on the banks of the perfect creeks we toured, I mentioned to my guide that a six-foot 2-weight could be just as transportive and isolating a device as a Beaver de Havilland.

My nostalgia was in overdrive by the time we made the last stop of the day. This particular creek was a little bigger than the others. You couldn't quite jump across it, and there was intermittent room in the forest canopy for overhead casting. It also looked mighty fishy with its deep, slow bends clotted with wood, short riffles that sparkled in the sunlight, and dark undercuts where you'd never stick a hand. All in all, it was as if someone had taken the most interesting features of all the best small streams I had fished in my life and put them together in a tidy package.

"Trout need different habitats at different life stages," my guide explained. I jotted that down in my notebook and below it added: *Anglers too.*

Under pretense of taking photos, I mentioned that I was going to walk the creek up to the first private property line. All was quiet and still. High overhead, pine boughs sifted the late-afternoon sunlight until it fell like a soft powder on the stream. Deer droppings glistened like coffee beans on the crisscrossing game trails. At one point I bent down and dipped my finger in the creek to check the temperature (it was cold-cold), and a brook trout untucked itself from a root wad and stitched its way upstream. I stared at the spot it disappeared to for a few minutes, a long ribbon of water in honeyed light.

Then I looked up.

Pink wisps of flagging tape hung from the low branches of a tree. They flickered in front of a dirty wooden board. On it were painted two words: *For Sale*.

III.

Human lives tend to move from a place of common experience to one of great divergence. Everyone starts out with diapers and dairy, but by the time you reach the age of 35, there's a fair amount of diversity. Retired athletes are buying their first car franchises. Former poli-sci majors are making runs for public office. Certain writers are entering the cushy and remunerative keynote-speaker eras of their careers. And then there was me, pitching a tent on two feet of fresh April snow next to a caved-in '60s travel camper, an unknown creek flowing past my feet.

I was taking a major gamble on this water. No one I spoke with could tell me much about it. The World Wide Web had told me zilch. The only actionable data I had on it came from a quick walkabout with the Realtor, during which I'd seen one good-size brown trout dart out of a cutbank. But it was the only parcel I could afford, due to the fact that its 90-year-old owner was on his last legs and his children wanted it gone before he passed. It still required me to dump all the actual and theoretical money I had into it, bypassing banks and instead taking out a high-interest personal loan, but by Christmas it was mine. And though I was excited, I was also terrified. What if the creek didn't fish well? What if it didn't satisfy? Would I come to regret that I'd turned down summer trips to the Kola Peninsula and Mongolia in order to explore the creek in its entirety? Was I making the biggest mistake of my life?

My anxiety would not be allayed with any sort of expedition. It was a colder-than-normal spring, and anyways the creek was the sort of icy system that doesn't start fishing well until the world really warms up. By the time mid-May rolled around, there were still patches of snow in the pines. The fishing was slow. I tallied a few small fish nymphing, but those didn't count. I hadn't gotten a place on the water to float bobbers. I wanted my summers to have wings.

Then there befell the creek one of those rare meteorological feats that sometimes happens in springtime, a ninety-degree day that was destined for July or August but had blown off course and made an emergency landing before Memorial Day. I knew from experience that the year's first hot spell generally does something tremendous to the bug life on an icy creek. Detonate is not too strong a word. This heat wave would act, I knew, like a kind of MRI of the river. That evening a full and comprehensive health exam would be completed, and my great genius or terrible folly would at last be revealed.

I finished my chores early and got on the water when the sun was still a few hands high of the tallest white pine. Sure enough, what had been an irregular pulse of sulfurs in the days prior slowly strengthened into a steady drip, and by early dusk a full fleet of little yellow sailboats was curling around my legs. Smaller fish started rising first, then slightly better fish. Spiders weaved meat traps in the alder branches. Waxwings swung from bank to bank as if hanging invisible garlands. The entire creek ecosystem was coming alive.

I started to catch fish on sulfurs, good creek fish in the thirteen-to-fourteen-inch class. But it wasn't until the sun dropped behind the trees that the mahogany spinners that had been hovering above my head all evening started to fall, and larger snouts began poking through the film. I turned a corner and was studying how to approach a pod of rising fish when I was startled by a sound all dry fly anglers live for, the baritone *thunk* that comes from a big head rising and falling. It was just a few yards upstream of me, such a hefty trout I could feel the eat in my chest, like a grouse's wingbeat.

I tried to measure my breathing but was only partially successful. When I brought my hands forth to add stronger tippet, they were full of tremors. "Hatch hands" I've always called them. If you get them, you know you are only partly in control of your life. You spend all your money traveling to fish, and then you spend all your money not traveling to fish. You tie multiple emerger, spinner, and dun patterns for each bug under the sun, and most of these flies you will never cast. But it's all worth it, because when a good trout rises to your offering, you feel like you've made a star shoot across the sky.

The giant trout ate on the first drift. I set the hook into weight, and that weight bolted upstream into a cavern of cedars. But the fight was over before I could give chase. One second my rod tip was arcing into the water, the next it was catapulting back to me, waving busted tippet in defeat.

But I was not disappointed to have lost that fish. Instead, a stupid smile split my face in half. And as I tied on a fresh fly in the red glow of my red lamp, I thought, *This is going to turn out all right.*

IV.

Three years have passed now since that fish, that season. Three seasons on the creek. As I try to finish this essay, I am sitting in an old camper I bought in rural Indiana for a song, a forty-foot Hy-liner with grandmotherly cupboards and a rotary phone. Nothing in it actually works the way it should, but I have installed a small woodstove that's good for heat and cooking. I run creek water through a gravity filter for coffee and general hydration. It suits me just fine.

Out the window of the camper there is an orchard I planted, fenced off from deer with landscaping pavers and chicken wire. The apple, cherry, and pear trees are blossoming; this might be the first year they give fruit. Even if they don't, there's plenty of wild food to be foraged. The cabinets in the kitchen are full of maple syrup and huckleberry jam. In a row of mason jars, dried honey fungus waits to be stewed with the next deer I arrow from the creek bottom.

Past the orchard sits a small Amish barn, a gift from my parents that functioned as a reception hall for my wedding. Somehow I met the sort of person I had never dreamed existed, a beautiful bug-obsessed girl who loved the creek so much she insisted we get married on its banks; we did, on a makeshift dock as the water tinkled by, then spent the next day drinking wine and watching strange blue midges dance above us, marveling at our cosmic luck.

My Nick Adams game is also much improved. I don't use it so much at bedtime—sleep comes too easily for that—but it is excellent recourse during monthly department meetings at the university. I wader up quietly as the PowerPoint presentation comes on, walk the fern-lined path past where the woodcock sits still as a carving over her clutch of blue eggs, sometimes pausing to pick a few serviceberries if they are ripe, sometimes startling a fawn in the tall grass. I always enter the creek in the same spot, right next to the leaning white pine with its broken Jenga tower of a tree stand.

There's usually only enough time to fish up to the dark seep where the swamp enters before I have to hurry back. During most excursions I only catch one or two fish—only rarely will I catch three—but once during budget discussions I caught five giant trout without moving my feet. When I time things correctly, I am out of my waders by the time clapping commences and the lights come back on, but some-times if I am working a good fish, or find a clump of thimbleberries, or follow a set of buck rubs deep into the alders, I don't get back until the middle of Q and A. After such tardy returns I eye my colleagues to my left and right nervously as I lean forward in my seat, checking to make sure I've removed my lanyard, feeling around under my chair for puddling water, hoping no one can smell the river on me.

CHAPTER 17

Why We Bass

MY FISHING INTERESTS TEND TOWARD THE MASOCHISTIC. MY IDEA of a perfect night on the river is one that sends me, face red and ears steaming, straight from the water to the vise to plot the following night's revenge. Blind casting for muskies till my hands turn to hamburger is very much my idea of a good time. I love to fish steelhead, but only after there's a few feet of snow on the banks and a few inches of ice in my beard. As I write these words, I'm preparing to spend the month of August bow-and-arrow casting tricos on a creek so brushed in you'd need a divining rod to find it.

Thank God I also love bass fishing.

Bass fishing—more specifically smallmouth bass fishing—is where I allow myself to bask in the pure pleasure of the angling enterprise, to kick back, relax, and finally do that one thing that for many anglers is the *only* goal: have fun. I was certainly due. Because of the pandemic it had been two years since I'd gone bassing in my very favorite place to do so: the freestone rivers of Northern Wisconsin. And so I plotted a spring trip, one that would also serve to give my wife, Amber, a tour of all those rivers I had fished before we had met. My old stomping grounds.

"It'll be fun," I assured her, though I immediately regretted my word choice. That word—*fun*—had not been in good stead ever since I had recently used it to describe her first fly-casting lesson . . . and the hatch-masking spinner fall that attended it.

"What's so fun about bass fishing?" she asked, suspicious.

I paused. It was a good question. There are pain indices galore, but how does one measure its opposite? How does one quantify pleasure? And how does one describe, to the uninitiated, the rare and unique experience of fishing smallmouth bass in the cradle of smallmouth civilization?

⟡

You know you're in Wisconsin when the gas station has six kinds of cheese curds and the woman behind you is carrying an armful of summer sausage like a stack of firewood.

"What's that blue thing?" she asked from behind the mountain of meat.

I looked at the window toward where she was pointing with her nose and saw that she was referring to my blue Aire raft. While it wouldn't turn a head in Colorado, river rafts are a rarity in Wisconsin, which as a whole is extremely walleye-oriented. To wit, the car filling up ahead of me was towing a deep V Lund with a kicker.

"It's a raft," I said, then clarified: "For fishing shallow rivers for smallmouth."

"Smallmouth are the best," she said, her head nodding in approval behind the top log.

"You got that right."

And she did. But how right? During the long drive with Amber through the Upper Peninsula I had been thinking long and hard about fishing and joy and a certain philosopher from my student days—the English utilitarian Jeremy Bentham—who had invented an algorithm for quantifying pleasure. He called it the *felicific calculus*, and while I am generally skeptical of *any* academic's ability to experience pleasure, I was curious enough to see if it might help me summon a description of smallmouth fishing that was richer than "flippin' awesome."

The timing of our trip was deliberate. I wanted Amber to see Wisconsin in its most splendid regalia, and a northern freestoner in the month of May is indeed a grand spectacle of flesh, with biomass that will give even coastal Alaska a run for its money. Whereas the Final Frontier has every make and model of Pacific salmon, the Dairy State boasts the full spectrum of suckers, and Packerland may even hold the trump card in the form of migratory sturgeon. I'd told Amber we were guaranteed to see a few, if not a few hundred, of these dinosaurs swimming in shallow water right under our kayaks. But there was another reason I wanted a spring trip, and that's because it's my favorite time of year to fish smallmouth bass. Those first few days of fishing bass after a long winter, when the fish shake off their torpor and become gluttonous spring torpedoes, are like the first few bites of pork belly the minute it leaves the smoker. In a word, perfection.

Our first float commenced on one of my favorite rivers in the world, a little-fished treasure dressed to the nines with glacial drift from the last ice age. You'd never know it by looking at the surrounding farmland, long cleared of its rocks and stones, but the rivers in this part of the world are full of long riffles and sparkling rapids littered with car-size boulders. We didn't have to wait long into our first float for the glut of finned flesh to make a full display. The launch of our kayaks sent redhorse suckers blasting through riffles and spraying our sunglasses, and before we turned the first bend, two sturgeon gracefully cleared a sandbar and disappeared into the depths, tails strikingly thin compared to their great wide heads. And while it couldn't be seen as easily, I knew that there was another key migration underway—that of *Micropterus dolomieu*. Many smallmouth bass rivers across the U.S. are heavily impounded, severely limiting bass movement, but on undammed freestone rivers, smallmouth flex their migratory instincts, traveling upward of 100 miles annually between deep downriver wintering areas and spring and summer holding water. There is even anecdotal evidence that individual fish return to the exact same two-foot by two-foot beds to spawn. Not for naught do some experts refer to smallmouth bass as warmwater salmon.

We spent the first hour slaloming through riffles and boulder fields in our kayaks, enjoying the perfect spring day, with the skies a cloudless blue and the bankside foliage still in that earliest fluorescence of green. As I looked for a suitable spot to start wade-fishing I considered the first vector in Bentham's calculus: *propinquity, or how soon the pleasure will occur*. I had to admit as I dipped my fingers in the water—it was cold and *barely* on its way to cool—that I wasn't entirely sure of how close we were to the first bass of the trip. What had started as a very warm spring had become in the week prior to our trip a very cold one. I knew we'd have excellent fishing by week's end—the forecast *did* call for steadily rising temps—but I was unsure how long we'd have to wait. An hour? A day? Two?

We pulled ashore on a midstream island that overlooked a long, slow feeding flat—the very sort of space where early season smallmouth would be soaking up some solar heat. I lost two flies to pike before tying on a wire leader, and then fished for a half hour before catching my first bass of the trip, a healthy fifteen-inch specimen that oozed slowly out of a deadfall and ate my fly on a long pause. A voracious attack this was not. I knew the cold water meant that the bass's metabolism would be in low gear, which meant, in terms of Bentham's *propinquity*, that the pleasure of these spring bass on any given cast was not as close as it would be on, say, an August afternoon. Instead of taking advantage of the bite window and immediately catching another fish—instead of doubling down on my fun, in other words—I first removed my waterproof notebook and made a few notes. Did I mention I'm an academic?

The next vector of happiness to interrogate was the *purity* of the experience, which Bentham defines as *the probability that the pleasure will not be followed by sensations of the opposite kind*. I wondered: *What on Earth was the opposite of smallmouth bass fishing?* Smallmouth floats, or at least the smallmouth floats I insist on, are beautiful things, full of sparkling rapids, lazy boulder gardens, towering hardwoods, and circling eagles. In short, they are beautiful experiences no matter where you look. So I tried to think of the ugliest places that I knew and eventually landed on the East Chicago steelworks I used to see as a kid while riding the Amtrak out of town. Next, I tasked myself with identifying finding the opposite of a smallmouth's fight on a fly rod, which is all electricity, and settled on the numbing act of grading two dozen freshman composition papers. Switching to a leech pattern, I caught two fish from a deep slot, one of which was almost revved up enough to jump. After releasing the second fish, I scanned the horizon: no belching smokestacks. I checked my calendar: no grading for four months. I removed my notebook and after the word *purity* wrote the words *exceedingly high*.

"Stop working!" Amber yelled. She was curving her kayak in a wide circle, trying to herd in a murder of sturgeon. She had, as usual, the right idea.

That evening some cloud cover settled in, which led to relatively high nighttime temperatures, which led to me waking up with a serious itch to get back on the water. "That's the thing about pre-spawn smallmouth," I said to Bentham in the imaginary dialogue going on in my head. "The fishing only gets better." As Amber and I had breakfast, I was riding high on what the philosopher identified as the vector of *certainty, or how likely or unlikely it is that the pleasure will occur*. With the first eighty-degree day of the year about to make landfall, I was certain of good fishing no matter what river we floated. This confidence existed in great contradistinction to my typical spring trout trip back home in Michigan, where my anxiety about where to fish can be so great I use a defunct rotary phone in my camper as a crystal ball, dialing 1-800-BIG-TROUT and listening to the cosmic murmurs coming in just below my tinnitus. This is not a joke.

For this next day of fishing, my brother would be joining us, with he and I fishing from the raft and Amber trailing behind in the kayak on what she was now calling a "sturgeon safari." With my brother on the oars, it was time to more fully interrogate that part of the felicific calculus that Bentham calls *the intensity of the pleasure*. I decided, for purposes of measurement, that one of the biggest sources of fishing pleasure, for me at least, comes from the drama of the eat. Now plenty of fish have exciting eats, it's true, but few boast as great a range of attacks as does the bronze bass. Brown trout and pike come quickly and slashingly to a streamer, and while bass will certainly do that, they will also leisurely trail a fly like a steelhead behind a swung offering, which interval creates an even unbearable sense of anticipation.

We had an early lunch under shade to escape the soaring heat, which created an uptick in dragonfly activity and an upswing in water temps. As I fished a few cheese curds out of a wet bag of whey, a thought began worming its way through my brain. Fact: Over the next few miles, the river will widen and slow. Fact: There will be plenty of vegetation growing up between the cobble. Fact: A dragonfly just landed on your last cheese curd.

Finally the thought burst through.

You should be throwing a topwater.

I had never fished a topwater for smallmouth so early in the year and had not even mentioned the possibility of surface fishing to Amber. Had you asked me, I would have said there was a greater likelihood of battling a snowstorm than fishing a surface bug in early May in Northern Wisconsin. And yet here we were. I looked around the raft. The only presentation outfit I had, a 6-weight with floating line, was still in its tube. But it was time. My hands were not my own as I started fitting the ferrules together. They weren't shaking, exactly, but they were also not firmly under my control. I have always called this phenomenon "hatch hands," and they only happen when there is a deep certainty that fishing joy is imminent. I maintain that those anglers who do not experience hatch hands as a regular part of their fishing practice are either psychopathic or in the wrong sport.

I told Amber to hang tight to the raft for the next part of the program. "You're about to witness one of the most beautiful takes in the fishing kingdom," I told her. I tied on my most trusted bug, an iridescent foam wiggly pattern developed by a friend of mine. It's constructed on a thin-wire hook and lands very softly, even as it presents a substantial silhouette. This particular fly was chafed and frayed from battle, and had even lost a leg or two, but it had the most important thing when it comes to conjuring one's first surface eat of the year: mojo. I made a long cast onto a feeding flat with a single boulder for cover.

"The take will be beyond subtle," I said to Amber as we both watched my fly.

Correction: We tried to watch it.

"Where is it?" Amber asked.

My fly, indeed, was nowhere to be seen. I looked behind me, thinking a frayed tippet had released it on the backcast, but it wasn't there either. Then I noticed that my fly line was moving—in the opposite direction of the current.

While a good bass can take you for a run on an 8-weight, and will keep you very honest with a 7-weight, it takes care, finesse, and a bit of luck to land a good fish on a 6-weight in skinny water, where the only direction for escape is the sky. *How long*, I could hear Bentham murmuring into my ear as the fish jumped once, twice, three times, *how long will the pleasure last?* Had we been in heavier flows we might have had to take up anchor, but instead my brother netted the fish after a glorious five-minute battle that left my forearm aching sweetly.

"And that," he said, holding the fish up for Amber, "is why we bass."

I rowed for the next hour. The river was wide and the fish were everywhere, which meant I barely even needed to steer as my brother cast from the bow. There was first-fish-on-top afterglow to be relished with cold beer, summer sausage, and squeaky curds. *The pleasure*, I critiqued Bentham between bites, *in certain situations compounds even after the cessation of the stimulus.*

The hours flew up and away, lost among the raptors, and before I knew it the evening sun was in my eyes, along with the only sight that could have saddened me: the bridge that was our takeout.

I wasn't ready. Not at all. I wanted more river, more hours, no rest or reset needed. Spring bass fishing was the purest possible expression of Bentham's final vector, his *fecundity, or the probability that the action will be followed by sensations of the same kind.* Perhaps there is no clearer affirmation about the joy of bassing than the fact that, had a genie popped out of my empty beer bottle, I would have asked for only more of the same. I'd tell him to throw the sun back up, to roll the river back out, to manifest more beer and more cheese. Only this time I'd put away the notebook. I'd stash the pen. When it comes to bassin', there's more joy than a philosopher can count.

CHAPTER 18

A Hex upon Me

"I haven't hexed in five years." Last fall I started mumbling this compulsively, like the ancient mariner who tells his tale to one in three, to anyone in my vicinity. I told my barber, my colleagues, my students, the latter of whom exchanged knowing glances with each other, their suspicions of madness finally confirmed. While it's anyone's guess how non-anglers understood my moaning—bewailing a hiatus from devil craft?—my fishing friends appreciated the depth and direness of the situation. To the Midwestern trout angler, the mayfly known as *Hexagenia limbata* is the universe's one clear compensation for our missing mountains, our absent ocean, the danger of moving through life knowing that, one day, you may be called upon to drive through Indiana. To miss the Winged Redeemer five years in a row points to an existential crisis that asks, *What, oh angler, are you doing with your life?*

The problem was that every year I seemed to get an irresistible assignment that coincided with hex time. There was the June I spent surrounded by thousands of puckering grayling in a Polish mountain valley smeared with wildflowers. The June I spent in Alaska swinging tiny headwater tributaries for un-tiny king salmon. The June I spent hammered by blackflies while hammering brook trout and Ouananiche in Labrador. But no matter how good the day at one of these far-flung destinations had been, when I went to bed each night, I was haunted by what I was missing back home in Michigan: giant, demon-eyed trout with spots as big as your fist; moonlit mudflats that went from calm to bubbling in the blink of an eye; the baritone *thunk* of a big trout rising in the dark, so resonant you could feel it in your chest, like a grouse's wingbeat. "Next year I fish hex," I would whisper to myself in the darkness after the camp generator was killed, or the northern lights glittered forth above a horizon of spruce. But then winter would come again, some exotic opportunity would drift into view, and like a spring brook trout I'd rise to it. Then one year I snapped. "No more," I declared. And just to show the universe how serious I was, I bought a trout camp.

It wasn't fancy and it wasn't huge, just a few acres at the end of a Michigan two track, undeveloped except for a rotted-out late '60s camper and two equally ancient picnic tables, their benches bowed like the tusks of a bull elephant. Across the south end of the property ran a small creek, and while it was too small and cold to support the great burrowing mayfly, it did flow into the mainstream of a bigger river just a half mile away. And what a stretch that was. There the big river took on a different character compared to the fifty or so miles of water above it. The cobble petered out to sand as the water widened and deepened, and pine forests yielded to black-dirt farmland. Total numbers of trout decreased while the average size ballooned, and locals spoke of the occasional walleye and pike. In short, it was twenty river miles of the most perfect hex water you could imagine, even if you were a professional dreamer with many empty hours to spare. In other words, a fishing writer.

I closed on the property in early December, which gave ample time to get my hex camp up and going, if not a lot of money with which to do it. Acquiring the camp had required all of my meager savings as well as a substantial, high-interest personal loan—about what you'd expect of a writing teacher living in a rental in an overpriced college town. Luckily, the past fifteen years of fishing and bushwacking meant I had everything I needed for a monastic dry fly existence. I had tarps galore, a tent for every season, a sleeping bag proven down to minus ten, water filtration systems great and small, and all the accouterments of an outdoor kitchen, right down to the manual coffee grinder. Perhaps most important, I was exceedingly wealthy in fly-tying materials, with a particularly robust portfolio of elk and moose assets, in addition to my ample rooster holdings. And so as deep winter set in I got to tying flies, focusing mainly on emergers and spinners, including the "twitch" spinners I like to prospect with during daylight hours. Every pattern I tied, I tied by the double dozen, since even the most sturdily reinforced hex imitation may come to resemble an exploded hummingbird after a good fish, and on a long night of steadily rising trout, you can expect to go through quite a few flies. "Quantity," Stalin observed of wartime foot soldiers, though it holds equally true of a hex box, "has a quality all its own."

On account of a late April blizzard that dropped twenty-six inches on top of an already ample Northwoods snowpack, it wasn't until the second week of May that I was able to drive back to camp and start getting it into shape, though work, per the longstanding contract I held with myself, was limited to those hours absent of bug activity. Still, in between fishing caddis, Hendricksons, mahoganies, and sulfurs, I managed several key improvements, replacing the cracked slabs of my picnic tables (one became a fly-tying station, the other a propane-powered bistro), assembling a large kindling pile of jack pine and cedar branches (they supported the face cord of ash a wood-wealthy friend contributed), and tarping out a living area amidst a copse of black cherries (it seated five comfortably and was rated to wind gusts of 40 mph). I sprung for one new item, a molded plastic rafting toilet that I plopped square in the center of a huckleberry patch beside an elegant wooden coatrack one of my downstate neighbors had left at the curb. This most refined area of camp I dubbed The Gentleman's Club and could one day see it featuring walls, a roof, and a cigar bar, though for now a roll of toilet paper in a Ziploc bag would have to suffice.

By the middle of June my hex camp was both complete and completely bereft of creature comforts, which is to say it existed to totally support, and in no way distract from, ardent fishing. Satisfied, I drove out to the hilltop that offered the only cell signal for ten miles and texted directions and an open invitation to all my fishing friends, from Minnesota to Georgia. And then it was time to commence The Watch.

A fawn sloshing through a shallow riffle. A single file of baby rac-coons following mama through the alders. All the sets of unblinking eyes, large and small, watching you from the woods. I'd forgotten how strange and beautiful it is to row a boat through the darkness with freshly greased oarlocks, silent as a drifting log, straining your ears in the darkness for the sound of a good fish feeding. After a few nights in the dark I could feel my old nocturnal form returning. Like a snowshoe hare adapts to its winter surroundings, I commenced a series of phys-iological changes. My night vision improved to the point where all I needed was starlight to guide the boat downstream, and a full moon had me wanting sunglasses. My hearing became so sensitive I could tell the size, location, and general structure of a logjam by the tinkling sound it made in the current. My olfactory system honed itself to the point of prophecy; I could smell the sweet rot of a slow hex-incubating stretch of river from two bends away. And my circadian rhythms shifted such that my energy was no longer fading with the sun, but rising with the moon. The cycling yelps of the whip-poor-will, which till now had signaled the end of the fishing day, now portended the beginning.

But five days into The Watch I hadn't seen a single *Hexagenia*. Naturally. Suffering through a fair amount of nothing is necessary to be there for the beginning of anything, and anglers looking to fish the hatch from tip to tail must be ready to pass some empty nights indeed. But the effort is worth it. There's a singular enchantment that comes from being there when the first wave of faintly luminescent nymphs decide, according to their private reasons, to wriggle free of their gray shucks and stretch their glowing wingtips toward the glowing moon. And because human beings haven't yet pinpointed the exact combi-nation of water and weather that births the great bug, being present on the first hex night requires painful patience and numbing sacrifice. But the spoils of the early hatch are grand: rivers empty of other anglers, and fish who'll eat just about anything you cast.

The day my scouting missions struck gold was, for the record, June 21st. The sky's last faint purple smear had just gone black as I turned a bend and glided onto the same long, calm straightaway I'd loitered at for the previous two nights, for no other reason than it had the best acoustics for ten river miles and would allow me to hear a rise from a great distance. I dropped anchor and waited. Though I was hungry, I dared not munch the apple at my feet, which might drown out the sound of a sipping trout. A few bats squeaked about as full dark settled in. The moon peaked over the treetops, glazing the river in a silver trim.

Then I heard it.

The rise was faint but unmistakable, still at least forty yards downstream and likely more, the heady *bloomp* of a large trout. Quietly, I drew anchor and slipped downstream, straining my eyes at the black water. Sure enough, there was a trickle of large mayflies glowing pale yellow in the moonlight, their wings pointed and erect, as if the river had sprouted teeth.

I felt all the old hex feeling.

The fish in question seemed to be eating flush against the bank, presumably beneath overhanging vegetation. It was the kind of outsize specimen that you never otherwise saw or caught, and yet here it was, suddenly manifest, thumping its slow drum in the dark. I exited the boat upstream in the deeper water of the channel, then waded slowly along the shallow bank until I was within ten yards of the trout, careful not to get too close. By this point the rhythm of its rising had picked up just a little to about twice a minute. When it ate, the ring of the rise licked moonlight.

After the next rise, I counted to twenty and cast. The presentation felt on point, and I tracked the fly with my peripherals, a faint orb oozing downstream. When it entered the trout's vector, I heard a *bloomp*.

I set the hook into great weight and the fish immediately started thrashing. It was bigger than I expected, but I applied just enough pressure to keep it from burying itself in the timber that clotted the main channel. After two hard runs it appeared in the beam of my headlamp, an angry apparition with markings as crisp as an ocelot's.

I released the fish quickly and got back to listening. The water was calm around my position and if I stared hard enough, I could make out the reflections of stars on the water. A dun passed through a nameless constellation, bobbed around my kneecaps, and disappeared into the dark beyond. A few seconds later I heard another good rise.

I blew on my fly as I crept downstream in the dark. It was going to be a good year.

~ ~

Thus did one of the greatest hex seasons of my life begin. I fished by myself, eating apples and sipping water. I fished with friends, eating sausage and drinking Scotch. Sometimes I covered seven miles in the boat, other times a hundred yards on foot. The bad nights were all alike; every good night was good in its own way. There was the night of the first great spinner fall, snouts poking skyward in every calm pool as if the trout were trying to stitch the moon's reflection to the water. There was the cold drizzly evening we almost stayed in our tents but instead dressed in winter layers and enjoyed our best night of the year, with bugs still twitching like wind-up bath toys when we reached the takeout at 4am. There was the night of midwifery when we scooped squirming nymphs up in our hands and watched them clear their shucks in our very palms, so in awe we forgot to fish. There was the night of the new moon when we ran aground six times but still had a night so prolific that we kept score on an old canoe paddle we found on the bank: *Dave K, 20. Rob R, 21.5. Tom H, 20.5.*

Fishing parties came and went. Moons rose and set. Dinner disappeared from life's daily cadence; breakfast joined forces with lunch. Then one day after the 4th of July, after the last crew of visitors had bidden their farewells, I awoke in my tent to something jarring—morning heat. By early afternoon it was blazing hot. For lunch I opened a cardboard box of soup and ate it as is, then drank a cup of coffee that never cooled. With no other worldly recourse, I spent the day alternating between wallows in the creek and spells in the hammock. Time dragged. Five hours before it was time to go to the river. Four hours. Three and a half. Three and a quarter. Three.

By this point in my hex journey, I had accomplished just about every goal I had. I'd caught my largest dry fly trout three times over; I'd discovered new spots to further explore and had noted areas to never fish again. The sane observer would be correct in wondering why I didn't declare victory, break camp, and return to civilian life. But absolute hexing corrupts absolutely. The same force that prevents you from leaving a large fish rising in the dark, though it's in an impossible spot and has ignored your flies for hours, is the same that prevents you from breaking down your rods, packing the Jeep, and heading home. Rather than satiate, the conveyor belt of big flies and big fish inspires a greater gluttony. Instead of patting yourself on the back for your best trout in years, you wring your hands and wonder: *Is tonight the night I lay hands on the fish of a lifetime?*

Around 5pm the light started to soften and the temperature eased. It was time to suit up. Without friends around I began my self-shuttle procedure, anchoring my boat at the put-in, driving the dirt road to the takeout, and walking the dusty road back in my waders, a journey of roughly one hour. It was a jaunt I had enjoyed the handful of times I'd done it, but on this day I felt myself starting to drag. One mile in, a painful blister I did not know I had burst and wept into my crusty sock. Looking for a stick to help with my limp, I fell backward into blackberry brambles. An entire fleet of logging trucks rumbled by, raising so much dust I almost dry-drowned. While taking a water break, I came across a turtle who'd met a gruesome vehicular fate, its shell shattered in dozens of pieces. Toeing the shards back together, it struck me that I was looking into a metaphysical mirror of sorts, that after three weeks of solid hexing I was equally frazzled, fractured, and spent.

In the boat the situation did not improve. My right shoulder developed a painful click that required a modified stroke, and the oarlocks, naked of grease, brayed like a pair of donkeys. On top of all that, the bugs that night were very sparse. Only a few smaller fish rose. Dunking my finger into the water, I winced: It was getting dangerously warm for trout. The one fish I caught was so exhausted from the ordeal that it took several minutes to revive him. When it finally swam off—to a rich and fruitful life, I hoped and prayed—the river had gone totally dead. And yet it was only midnight. I had five hours of river yet to row.

Dawn was blooming nectarine over the treetops when the landing came into view. I hooked up my boat and dragged it out of the inky black water one last time, my taillights so caked in dirt they barely glowed. It was over. I was done. Before heading back to camp I stood there for a few final moments, taking it all in. Morning birds chased each other from bough to bough. Two does swam across the river far downstream, heading back to bedding. A military truck rumbled off in the distance. Life after hex was about to get very different. I was going to bathe in something that wasn't a creek and sleep on something more than two feet wide. I'd wear comfortable shoes with clean socks and walk absentmindedly on beautiful flat pavement, no need to pick my step over rocks and root wads. There would be no fishing for a while, probably till the small wings of August, and I was ok with all that. Even more than ok. I felt downright giddy. And that's the thing about the hex hatch: You know you've done it right when you're glad it's over.

CHAPTER 19

So Long on Long Island

I.

Under the antiseptic light of the doctor's office, in a loose-fitting purple hospital gown, Amber shifts on the noisy wax paper that lines the bed, swinging her bare feet in the air. I sit in a chair a few feet away, still wearing my winter coat, my boots melting so much snow I've built a nest of paper towels beneath them. But the water is still pooling.

She is—we are—four months pregnant, and this is just a standard-issue checkup, the usual medley of weight, blood pressure, and sonogram.

But we also have another question for the doctor. A fishing question. Sort of.

"We're thinking about going on a trip," Amber says to the doctor after we finish discussing test results, all normal, all good.

"Ooh, babymoon," the doctor nods. "Where to and when?"

"The Bahamas at the end of March."

"Let's see," she says, looking at her calendar. "You'll be right at the edge of your second trimester by then, and we don't recommend any air travel during the third. But everything is going great, so I think that should be fine. Enjoy yourselves."

We walk across the icy parking lot to the truck. I hold Amber's hand, and we take it mincingly slow.

"What do you think she meant by 'on the edge?'" I say.

"Just that we wouldn't want to wait any longer," Amber replies. "And we're not. We're in great shape. I can't wait!"

We get in the truck and let it warm up a bit. Amber's cheeks are flush and there's a happy, faraway look in her eye. She's dreaming of sun and beaches, and you can't blame her. It's February in Michigan, after all, when the sun is not a regular customer of any sort, and a part of you fears it will never make heat again. That might be part of the reason we've chosen the name Summer for the baby—something light and bright for when the world isn't.

I myself feel a little more trepidation about our travels, not sure if the doctor knows exactly what Bahamas she has signed off on, mostly because I do not know exactly what Bahamas I have signed up for. We are going because I've taken a gig as writer and consultant for a fly-fishing startup, and Amber is my plus-one on a work trip—to the degree that fishing for bonefish while brainstorming how to grow a fishing company can be called work.

"We'll need our own place," I say. "It's going to be a pretty full house."

"Way ahead of you," she says, eyes on her phone.

I have never heard the word "babymoon" before last month, but I like the idea. And since Amber and I never had a proper honeymoon, getting married as we did at the height of Covid, it will be that too. But this trip is also something else, something private that I cannot share with anyone and that there isn't a word for. This would be, I knew, the last fishing I'd do before becoming a father and thus the formal end of an era in my life when I was free to prioritize my time on the water over all else. I did not know what the next fish after Summer's arrival would be, when it would happen, what it would feel like, and whether it would still hold the same meaning to me as before. I suspected my relationship to water, and in turn my relationship to myself, would change in some fundamental way, but I did not know how, exactly. So this trip—honeymoon, babymoon, work trip—is also a kind of farewell to a person I had been for a long time and would likely not ever be again. A goodbye moon?

Whatever it was, because I have identified as a fishing writer to the IRS for fifteen years, it would also be a tax deduction.

"I found the perfect Airbnb," Amber says, showing me her phone at a stoplight.

I gulp.

A very large tax deduction.

II.

I have never fished the salt. During my travel heyday, when I was single and without mortgage, and outdoor media still revolved around the printed word, I always thought that a saltwater invitation would manifest alongside all the many other fishing opportunities, which were so abundant that I could be selective about what assignments I took on. "Just wait until you fish the salt," people would say. "It'll change your life." I was curious what about they meant, since fly fishing had already been the primary shaping force of my 20s and 30s. My job teaching college writing? It was bad for pay, great for time off. Relationships? They were usually winter-only things. Housing? I hunted down eight-month leases—no sense in paying summer rent when you're basically living on the river. How then, I wondered, could this already very fishy life be further changed? But despite my desire to observe the alchemy of self and surf, no bonefish or permit or tarpon trip ever happened.

Now, eating fries with Amber in the food court of the Nassau airport, waiting to board one of the three flights a week the airline devoted to Long Island, with saltwater fishing finally—finally—in the offing, I am in a much different place. My life over the last two years has changed in ways so vast and profound that I feel any saltwater epiphanies will be lost in the noise. First, I got married. Then Amber and I bought a small house on a large tract of land with a chestnut orchard up front, a creek in the back, and a horse pasture in the middle. On top of all that we conceived a child, already the size of a mango.

Change my life? Go ahead and try, bonefish.

We finish eating, lounge around for another hour, and then it's finally time to walk across the tarmac to make the final leg of our journey. The vessel that will take us to Long Island is a small plane, a puddle jumper whose twin props are already blaring as we walk up the rickety staircase. It's painted in bright island colors, greens and yellows, which is probably why I don't recognize it until I'm inside sitting down. But looking up at the cockpit, I realize I have been in this very model of plane before. But where?

"George River," I blurt out to Amber.

"What?" she yells over the engine noise.

"I've been on a plane like this before. Northern Quebec. Atlantic salmon."

Yes, that was it. The interior of that plane had been configured differently, however. Where Amber sits, the seats had been stripped for a cargo area that held crates of potatoes, bacon, and flour, and in front of the cockpit had been a beaver dam of rod tubes. We'd flown low, almost too low, over the barrens of subarctic Quebec, watching black bear and caribou scamper below the shadow of the plane as it scrolled over the tundra. And when we finally landed beside the silver vein of the George River, it was with the icy Torngat Mountains looming in the distance.

This ride is a good deal different. Our plane is full of human cargo only—six of us, to be precise. And there is definitely no ice on the horizon, only blue water with island-size puddles of sunlight. After one hour we spy land, mostly green, very sparsely settled. In that sense, even though I have never been to the Bahamas or even the Caribbean, it feels familiar—remote and therefore fishy. Sometimes I feel like the sport of fly fishing is simply an excuse to get as far away as possible from as many people as possible. And while on past trips I've always embraced this sequestration from the world proper, as we land I can't help but think about the cost of this solitude. If there was, God forbid, an emergency, it would not be cheap or easy—or maybe even possible—to get off the island quickly.

We land and get our bags. The one-room concrete building that serves as front desk and baggage claim takes the gold medal for smallest airport I have ever been to, beating Esquel, Argentina, by a hair.

"Where is the car rental place?" Amber asks as we trundle our bags across the tarmac.

"The owner said she'd meet us here." "Here" being a small parking lot surrounded by a wire fence and then palm trees. Just then a car pulls up. "David?" A smiling Bahamian woman waves a piece of paper with my name on it, an unnecessary gesture given we are the only two people in the parking lot, but welcome nonetheless.

She gives us directions to town and tells us to leave the car in the parking lot, keys in and unlocked, when we leave the following week. We thank her and drop her off up the road at another car. Our vehicle is not dissimilar from the one I learned to drive on—in 1996. Prior to the trip my biggest vehicular concern was my ability to drive on the opposite side of the road. Now I have anxiety about the car itself. Hubcaps held on with zip ties. Piebald tires ready to pop. Ants and sand in the backseat. The dashboard made of cardboard with a woodgrain wallpaper. I dare not lift it to see what lies beneath.

"Rustic," Amber smiles. She's traveled to her fair share of far-off places and can take a janky car in stride, even while pregnant, and I smile a private smile that I lucked out in the cosmic lottery with this beautiful, adventurous wife.

An hour and four goat crossings later, we stop at the bodega our Airbnb host has recommended. I grab water, milk and cereal, and bananas, but we also need food-food, and the shopgirl directs me to an archipelago of rusty deep freezes in the back. They are full of frozen vacuum-sealed blocks of indeterminate content. No label, no date, no telling. I grab a week's worth of dinners.

"What did you get?" Amber asks.

I hold up a green and orange block of—something.

"We'll know when we know."

At the Airbnb we settle in and unpack. Amber stages her sun-bathing paraphernalia. I get my vise and fly-tying materials in position. There's a bottle of tequila from our hosts in the middle of the table and I avail myself of a tall glass as I set our first of six frozen mysteries to thaw in the sink.

Down on the beach the surf grabbles back on itself, blue water on bright sand. Amber pulls back her shirt to give Summer some air. The sun crackles on our pale midwinter skin. The view is prettier than any island postcard I have ever seen, nothing but water and rock and sand as far as the eye can see in both directions. Amber is beaming, calm and beautiful, and it's not lost on me that our previous fishing expeditions have been a little short on creature comforts, her last one resulting in the discovery of a blackfly allergy.

"Best fishing trip ever," she says.

III.

We spend a few days exploring the island, and then it's time for me to leave and meet the crew. "Don't worry about us," Amber assures me, rubbing her belly as I walk out the door. The company rental is a twenty-minute drive away on the other side of Deadman's Cay, and as I walk in there's music, fly-tying materials, beer and chips, and I am conscious, for the first time in my fishing life, of being an elder. But they are a welcoming and exuberant bunch, square in that stage of a fishing life when opportunity is maximal and responsibility minimal, a stage I am happy to revert to for the afternoon. They've been in town for about a week and are in a good groove of fishing the flats all day and soaking bait off the beach by firelight at night, which has resulted in a freezer full of shark and stingray. I've never had stingray before but it's delicious, with a texture like pulled pork. We eat it in tortillas with a papaya salsa before heading out fishing for the day.

"We haven't totally figured the program out, but we're getting there," Gil says as we stake out a place on the flats. We've been working together for months now, but so far all our encounters have been on Zoom. Up close and personal, I can tell how fishy he is, how much he loves being on the water. That's the one thing you can be sure of in the fly-fishing industry: No one is in it primarily for the money, and even those who make coin off the enterprise generally use it to fish more, or better, or maybe just differently. I myself started writing about fishing to stop being hassled by my mom and girlfriend about fishing so much. Fifteen years later, here we are.

After a short boat ride we arrive at our first spot of the day. I grab my 7-weight and jump out of the boat. The cork, I have to admit, feels a little awkward in my hands. In a normal March year, I'd already be a few thousand casts deep into streamer season, which is to say my shoulder would be agile, my hands callused, my forearms strong. But this is not March of a typical year. My body is not so much in fishing shape as it is in pasture-building form, and the strongest part of me right now is my back. And while I have calluses, they aren't in the right places, not on my palms but the creases of my fingers. The week prior to our departure, a deep freeze had caught us by surprise and frozen our hose line, which meant I'd been bringing the horses water in buckets—fifty gallons a day every day, and the pasture is a long walk from the hydrant.

Rust shows on my first opportunity, a barracuda. My fly falls so short of the fish it doesn't even notice. My second cast is on point though, and a few minutes later I am holding my first saltwater fish, one of the species of my childhood dreams, all teeth.

Our second spot feels fishier, a huge horseshoe of shallow sand with deeper water all around. The three of us—me, Gil, and his girlfriend, Jen—take up different positions and start watching. I'm standing at the base of the horseshoe, where you'd hold it if you were throwing it at a stake in a backyard game. Gil and Jen are each covering a tine. Nothing happens for a few minutes, but then, out of nowhere, three fish appear out of the deep, coming right at me. I drop a quick cast right in front of me. It feels too close, but the nearest bonefish drops its head and eats.

When the fish takes off I realize that everything I've been told about bonefish is true. The power in the first run is immense. It isn't an animal but a force of nature, not a fish but an engine.

"That's a really nice bone, man," Gil says. "Congrats."

"That was a ride and half," I smile, hands trembling a little.

More anglers join us in a second boat and we head out to explore new water. Fish come slowly at first, base hits in a well-pitched game, but then we stumble upon a long ditch connecting two different flats. It's deep, too deep to see the bottom. Sharks patrol just beneath the surface, big enough that we stay close to shore. One of the crew catches a fish from the deep slot. Then another. Soon we realize that there's a big group of bones schooled up just out of sight, maybe herded by the sharks. They aren't huge fish, but we catch one after another, doubles, triples, even one septuple with everyone's rod bent at once. The fishing is hot for about twenty minutes, and I lose count of how many I've landed. Then more sharks arrive, and the pool goes quiet.

We drink beers and talk. I am, I learn, the only one with a return ticket. No one is sure how long they'll stay. I know very well the feeling of an open-ended world, a float without a takeout, a river with no end. There are many worse ways to spend one's youth than fish, and very few better. "You all are doing it right," I say.

The sun is getting low and we lose our visuals, so we motor back to the house. It's time for a bonfire and the stingray rods, but I've got to get going. I say goodbye to the crew and get in the car, hoping that without Amber beside me I'll still remember to stay on the left side of the road.

Driving through the island twilight with the ocean on one side of me I think about the crew, with no idea when they were leaving. I think about Gil, who is considering buying a place on the island and anointing it company headquarters. In my past life I'd taken pains to stay just that kind of limber. Every fishing expedition was a trial period of a new life you could pursue if you so chose, every outing something that could be made to last forever, or at least for a few months. You could move to Anchorage, to Ennis. You could learn Spanish and migrate to Patagonia every winter. You could spend the next few years entirely devoted to the capture of muskellunge. You could follow the bugs from April to August, watch their wings getting bigger and bigger, then smaller and smaller.

That life now feels like a very long time ago. I am now the dictionary definition of not limber; life is no longer a trial period. I have a mortgage, a wife, a child on the way. I will not be spending the next few weeks looking up real estate in the Bahamas. I will not be reconfiguring my life in order to hunt the next fishing high, to chase the next new species, to embrace the next novel rush.

On the way home I stop at a bakery I have read about, to surprise Amber with something sweet. It is a simple, small place, with an array of pastries on a folding table. Beyond the table is a living room where a child clambers on an air mattress among a sea of stuffed animals. I wave at her and she waves back, smiling shyly. I clear my throat and Mom appears, looking tired, and rings me up. When she hands back my change the coins are covered in flour.

That will be us, I think. Soon. A little critter will occupy all our time and take all our energy while we tend to the storefront of our lives. I wave back at the little girl. She hides her face behind a raccoon and waves back. And suddenly I realize that during all those years of fishing I had kept myself limber in the other way, too, the non-fishing way. I hadn't quit my job at the university to live in my camper and fish full-time, even though I'd threated to do so a thousand times. I'd never canceled a flight home and guided the rest of a season. I'd stayed open to the life I now had, a veritable coup. I'd managed to fish my brains out for fifteen years and then, like the spy in the movie turning sideways to fit the elevator's closing doors, found a way to slip into a perfect little family life.

At our rental Amber is resting, windows open, curtains dancing, surf soughing.

"How was your day?" I ask.

She smiles dreamily, one hand low on her belly and one hand high. "Me and Summer went to the beach, had a snack, and then took a nap. Then we did it again."

"I brought banana bread."

"Yum!"

We eat and watch the sun set, close enough to the surf that we feel sprays with each big breaker.

"Are you two ready for tomorrow?" I ask.

"Yes, but we don't want to be in the sun for more than two hours."

"Two hours will be all we need."

IV.

The next morning after breakfast we begin to make preparations. We pack all the beach lounging standards—towels, water, food, sunscreen, hats—but this time I'm also packing along my 7-weight, flats sneakers, and fly box. This morning we are going fishing together. Our first family fishing trip.

We turn the piebald sedan off the main road onto a patch of jagged rock that I take very, very slowly. With no cell service we have to rely on some old written directions I've cribbed from a fishing website that looks like it was last updated in 1999. It feels just like when I'd first started exploring Northern Michigan, back in the day when phones were only for talking and you navigated the warrens of logging roads with only a few sentences, an odometer, and your wits. *At the first fork, turn right. Go .8 mile. At the third fork, turn left. In 1.3 miles turn right.* At times you felt like you were going in circles, that you would never arrive and be lost in the woods forever, but then the river would magically appear behind the cedars, and it was always the most perfect thing you'd ever seen.

Cresting a hilltop, we finally catch a glimpse of blue above the trees. We are going the right way. We stop to let a small herd of goats pass from one forest of shrubs to the other, but when we start forward again, the car falls sharply with a thump that feels like it could have done some damage. It's heavy enough that I get out to check the tires and under-carriage, which features so many white zip ties it looks like the car has worms.

Finally we park the car and walk a short goat path down to the water. I'm carrying a cooler, folding chair, water, and snacks. Amber carries Summer.

It's a big bowl of a flat, with land curving around it like a pair of protective arms and, far in the distance, a little inlet to the sea. I look for a place to set us up. The beach won't do. It's too rocky, and in any case I need Amber closer to me if we are going to execute our plan. So we wade out onto an ankle-deep flat and I set the chair and cooler in a few inches of water, displacing the world's smallest shark in the process.

"The water's not going to rise up suddenly, is it?"

"No. We're good for two hours. And then it will actually start falling back."

I rig up as Amber explains to the baby what we are doing here. "This is called fly fishing—" she begins. We—Amber and I—have been very deliberately and systematically exposing Summer to all those things we hold dear, in the hope of affecting some metaphysical transmission of affection or prowess or both. At month number six, we have thus far ensured that Summer will have the right to wear the following T-shirts:

"I've been riding horses since before I was born."

"I've been chasing chickens since before I was born."

"I've been following blood trails since before I was born."

"I've been listening to David Bowie since before I was born."

"I've been eating pierogi since before I was born."

The one action item missing?

"I've been fishing since before I was born."

It is, indeed, an egregious omission, but one I could not help due to the timing of the pregnancy. Summer had been conceived in October, and Amber was not donning waders in December to join me for winter steelheading. And her due date at the end of June meant any spring fishing would be even more impossible; no one's chasing sulfurs when there's a chance your water could break. So here we were.

Summer's first experience of fishing would be a Bahamian bonefish fest.

The flat here feels like a flooded desert, which I suppose is what flats are. I start to work my way out from Amber, moving slowly and looking for fish against the wobbling lattice of light, taking care that I never go so far away that I can't hear her yell or read her hand gestures. Within five minutes I spook two fish I should have caught. Then nothing for an hour. I am at this point a few hundred yards from Amber. This is the limit, I tell myself. It's time to turn around and start fishing my way back.

Then, of course, a large bonefish appears.

It's by itself and far enough off that it takes no note of me, beyond casting range but also moving slowly enough that I can keep pace if I hustle. I follow it up the bank, sometimes losing it for a few seconds but always finding it again. It disappears into the mangroves. It reappears on bright sand. I try a few times to close the distance enough to pull off a cast, but it's no dice. Amber is getting smaller and smaller and I suddenly realize I couldn't hear her now if she called out. I abandon the fish and start to wade back.

It takes about twenty minutes of walking, but I am an expert slosher, and it's much easier moving across this calm flat than it is a wood-clotted creek. I think of all the returns I have made, heading back alone to the truck or takeout, sometimes in glory, sometimes in defeat. In waders and in shorts. Winter, spring, summer, fall. Years, decades.

What did all those moments mean now? Would the things I'd learned and seen serve any purpose to the husband I'd become and the father I was becoming? Would all those fish I had caught or failed to catch prove to have some utility? Or would they exist as mere ornaments, personal souvenirs, little trinkets to turn over in my head when life got hard?

"Catching fish since before I was born?" Amber asks when I arrive.

"*Fishing* since before she was born," I say. "She'll have plenty of time to figure out the catching part."

V.

The last fish I would catch before becoming a father comes on the penultimate day of the trip. I am back with the crew for the morning. And not just the crew—a group of podcasters and videographers has arrived, and we are now nine strong, needing three boats to get around. We fish out the morning but by lunch one of the newcomers isn't looking so good. Whether it's food poisoning or heatstroke or the latest and greatest Covid variant is impossible to say. All we know is that one of the boats has to leave for the day, and whoever is on it won't be coming back out. We draw straws.

"It's his last day, so he's staying," Gil says, pointing at me. I don't protest. Everyone else will be fine, I know. They'll be here for another week. Maybe two. Maybe they'll never leave the island. But today I'll be making my last cast until—I sincerely don't know when.

I set off with a small group, including a freshly arrived drone operator. We have not yet found the land of bonefish milk and honey, so we hopscotch around from flat to flat. It's a lovely day with a steady, easy wind, and I can see very clearly the allure of this whole saltwater fishing thing. The drone operator looks like he's been whipping around the Caribbean for a while now, his skin deeply tanned and his attitude . . . very islandy.

The drone follows me for a bit as I fish. It's a familiar whirring sound—I have flown more than a few drones in my day. Over the last few years it had become increasingly necessary to collect diverse images for stories I was covering, so in addition to my Moleskine and Fischer Space Pen, I often toted two Pelican cases, one with standard camera gear and another, the drone. And while I always enjoyed taking photographs, I never did anything but despise the little flying robot. When it crash-landed in a river during my last shoot, taking a chunk of my thumb with it, I'd been thrilled. My client ran up and helped me fish it out of a logjam.

"Do you think it's ok?" he had asked.

"I sure hope not," I said.

After a time, the drone departs. It's about time for a fresh battery, if the pilot can find a decent place to land. He carefully lowers it onto the bottom of the boat, one propeller thwacking aluminum on the descent. I feel very happy that the sun is setting on one particular chapter of my fishing life and think back to a children's book we received as a baby shower gift, which I have been using to practice my goodnight stories.

"Goodnight, drone," I say to the empty air.

"Goodnight, editor whispering *rush*."

"Goodnight, deadlines everywhere."

The light starts to get low, which means we have time for one last spot. I haven't yet caught a fish today and am at peace with that. Still, one more would be nice.

I look up at the sky and repeat: One more would be nice.

We motor into a large wilderness of mangroves veined with channels running between little islands. Strong tidal currents here and there. A good place to hunt, for bonefish and bonefish angler alike.

I wander off as far as I can while still seeing the boat. I glimpse nothing, nothing, nothing for an hour. I open my last Kalik. The wind picks up, howls around me, pulls a little bit of music out of the bottle—almost but not quite the cooing Amber uses to talk to Summer.

And then I see something. Maybe. A slight aberration of light, far off and moving deeper into the flat, a wandering scrap of pale shadow. If it's a fish it's quartering steeply away, already at the limit of my casting and going farther out. I cast beyond myself, not a measured presentation but a half-blind heave. Somewhere in the indeterminate distance the fly lands. There's a *tap tap*. And then my reel is spinning in a blur as my fly line breaks for the horizon.

I hold fast to the cork as the drag whines and the fish flees, and suddenly I am six years old, flying a kite with my father, caught in that moment when the wind rips and grabs and all you can do is just stand there, index fingers in the tubes of the spool, trying to keep all other digits clear. Sometimes you got the kite back and sometimes you lost it.

A few minutes later the fish is at my feet. It's just me and him—it feels like a him—in the middle of this huge flat. The middle of the middle. Far from one shore, far from the other, in this strange space where lasts and firsts rub up against each other, ends and beginnings, goodbyes and hellos.

The bonefish, oblivious to all this hullabaloo, swims away, light and easy.

VI.

Our last full day Amber and I save for each other. We spend the morning making sure everything is as it needs to be—flight on schedule, horses and chickens still alive, ride home from the airport all lined up—then go to one last beach.

This one is at the southernmost tip of the island. There's a shack where we have our last meal of conch. We walk the beach. We laze in the shade. Then we go for one last long dip in the surf.

In the water the three of us ebb and flow with the waves, weightless. I trace a finger on Amber's belly, the small dome below which our fierce little girl waits for the world. Can she feel the sun? Hear the water? Smell the salt?

"I've been flying rickety planes since before I was born," Amber says.

"I've been eating conch fritters since before I was born."

"—Dodging goats since before I was born."

"—Squashing scorpions since before I was born."

We laugh and stretch back into the waves.

"We need to come back here someday," Amber says. "The three of us."

The statement catches me by surprise, but I like the sentiment. A lot.

"When she's 16," I reply. "When she can cast."

"Are you kidding? She'll be a great caster by the time she's 12."

"Twelve, it is. 2034. Book your ticket."

We float back and put our feet up, letting the waves rock us back against the beach, a kind of levitation. It isn't that far off, when you think about it. Only twelve years. Twelve years of firsts. The first time she'll watch a bobber bounce. The first time she'll feed her mamma and dadda a fish she caught. Her first rising trout.

The first horse she falls in love with. The first time it whips away at full gallop, snatching her breath.

And other firsts too. The ones she won't see coming and can't expect, wonders beyond what her mother and father could ever imagine, bright shapes in bright sun, swimming round and round, waiting for her reach.

Acknowledgments

I am indebted to a great many people for their support, counsel, friendship, and mentorship.

A hearty round of thanks to my writing teachers, who taught me the joy and power of the right word: Wendy Moss, Tim Scanlan, Monica Berlin, Robin Metz, Beth Ann Fennelly, Tom Franklin, Peter Ho Davies, Julie Orringer, Fred Busch, and Eileen Pollack.

A ream of gratitude to all my fishy mentors and collaborators, who shared their love of water and wild places with me: Igor Glinda, Arek Kubale, Mirek Pieślak, Charlie Piette, Tim Landwehr, Mike Schultz, Chris Willen, Misty Dhillon, Ethan Winchester, Tom Lynch, Tom Rosenbauer, Austin Adduci, Justin Witt, and Bob White.

A monumental thanks to the many editors I've worked with over the years, who provided so much direction and encouragement when it came to the craft of storytelling: Greg Thomas, Tom Bie, Kirk Deeter, Gil Greenberg, Sam Lungren, Paris Fleezanis, Zack Williams, Ross Purnell, Gerry Bethge, Alex Robinson, Steve Duda, Marshall Cutchin, Chad Shmukler, Jeff Smith, and Allison Jarrel.

To everyone I've ever shared a boat or sandbar with, especially Tom Hazelton, Jason Tucker, Erick Johnson, Greg Schutz, Rob Ramsburgh, Stevenson Ramsburgh, Brian Bergeson, Alex Cerveniak, and Brian Kozminski: thank you.

A ragamuffin writer doesn't travel around the world without quite a bit of material support, so I am exceedingly grateful to Scientific Angler, Orvis, YETI, SIMMS, and Far Bank for their generosity and sponsorship. An extra special shout-out to Kara Armano, without whom I might have had to chase mahseer with a 6-weight.

To the crew at Lyons Press—especially Eugene Brissie, Lynn Zelem, and Brooke Goode—who helped this mass of words achieve such handsome final form: a thousand thanks.

Everlasting gratitude to my parents, who encouraged me to live a life of adventure, and my brothers, the best fishing partners a guy could ask for.

And lastly, eternal and abiding thanks to my wife, Amber, and daughter, Summer, to whom this book is dedicated. None of this would have been possible without your love, support, and laughter.